KINDEST REGARDS

ALSO BY TED KOOSER
FROM COPPER CANYON PRESS

Splitting an Order

Delights & Shadows

Braided Creek: A Conversation in Poetry
(with Jim Harrison)

TED KOOSER

Kindest Regards

New and Selected Poems

 Copper Canyon Press
Port Townsend, Washington

Cover art: Don Williams, *Sonoma Street Corner,* oil on canvas, 14 × 16 in.

Copper Canyon Press is in residence at Fort Worden State Park in Port Townsend, Washington, under the auspices of Centrum. Centrum is a gathering place for artists and creative thinkers from around the world, students of all ages and backgrounds, and audiences seeking extraordinary cultural enrichment.

LIBRARY OF CONGRESS CATALOGING-IN-PUBLICATION DATA
Names: Kooser, Ted, author.
Title: Kindest regards : new and selected poems / Ted Kooser.
Description: Port Townsend, Washington : Copper Canyon Press, [2018]
Identifiers: LCCN 2017056274 | ISBN 9781556595332 (hardback : alk. paper)
Classification: LCC PS3561.O6 A6 2018 | DDC 811/.54—dc23
LC record available at https://lccn.loc.gov/2017056274

ISBN 9781556595349 (pbk.)

9 8 7 6 5 4 3 2 FIRST PRINTING

COPPER CANYON PRESS
Post Office Box 271
Port Townsend, Washington 98368

www.coppercanyonpress.org

To the memory of my parents, Ted and Vera

NOTES AND ACKNOWLEDGMENTS

Sure Signs: New and Selected Poems was published by the University of Pittsburgh Press in 1980, and contained what I and my editor, Ed Ochester, thought were the strongest and most representative poems from my earlier books and chapbooks, among them *Official Entry Blank* (University of Nebraska Press, 1969), *A Local Habitation & a Name* (Solo Press, 1974), and *Not Coming to Be Barked At* (Pentagram Press, 1976). I still stand by those choices, as I think Ed would, and this current volume's first section, from *Sure Signs,* is thus a selection from a 1980 selection. Thanks to the University of Pittsburgh Press for their permission to use poems from books they published, *Sure Signs, One World at a Time,* and *Weather Central.* The poems "A Heart of Gold" and "Barn Owl" first appeared in *Weather Central* and later in *Valentines.* I've included them in the selection of poems from *Valentines* here.

The poems in *The Blizzard Voices* are my verse arrangements of the recollections of survivors of the Great Blizzard of 1888, as recorded in newspapers of the period and later in local histories compiled in the early years of the twentieth century. I owe much to one volume in particular, *In All Its Fury,* compiled by W.H. O'Gara, published in 1947 by Union College Press, Lincoln, Nebraska. Thanks to the University of Nebraska Press for their permission to use these poems.

Thanks to Jerry Costanzo and Carnegie Mellon University Press for permission to include a selection of poems from *Winter Morning Walks: One Hundred Postcards to Jim Harrison.*

It has always been difficult for me to get far enough away from my own poems to see them clearly and objectively. While selecting work for this book I asked for the help of friends whose judgment I trust: James Crews, Phil Dentinger, Pat Emile, Dan Gerber, Jonathan Greene, Jon Munk, Maria Nazos, Connie Wanek, Michael Wiegers, my editor at Copper Canyon, and Chuck Woodard. And, as always, my wife, Kathleen Rutledge, has been of immeasurable help.

Some of the poems in the New Poems section were previously printed in the following journals: *Able Muse, Antioch Review, The Atlantic, Bellevue*

Literary Review, Connotation Press (Hoppenthaler's Congeries), *The Idaho Review, Jewish Journal, Kenyon Review, The Midwest Quarterly, Narrative, New Letters, New Ohio Review, Poetry East, Rattle, Solo, The Southern Quarterly, Southwest Review, Upstreet,* and *World Literature Today.*

The Stanley Kunitz quotation is from an October 12, 1997, interview with Mark Wunderlich for the Academy of American Poets and posted on poets.org.

PREVIOUS PUBLICATION CREDITS

"Selecting a Reader," "First Snow," "An Old Photograph," "The Constellation Orion," "The Salesman," "Old Soldiers' Home," "Fort Robinson," "How to Foretell a Change in the Weather," "Snow Fence," "In an Old Apple Orchard," "After the Funeral: Cleaning Out the Medicine Cabinet," "Carrie," "For a Friend, "Five P.M.," "Abandoned Farmhouse," "At the Bait Stand," "The Widow Lester," and "The Red Wing Church" from *Sure Signs: New and Selected Poems,* by Ted Kooser, © 1980. Reprinted by permission of the University of Pittsburgh Press.

"Flying at Night," "In the Basement of the Goodwill Store," "In January, 1962," "Father," "The Fan in the Window," "Daddy Longlegs," "Goodbye," "Laundry," "Ladder," "Walking at Noon near the Burlington Depot in Lincoln, Nebraska," "At Nightfall," "Cleaning a Bass," "A Letter," "The *Voyager 2* Satellite," "As the President Spoke," "The Urine Specimen," and "Porch Swing in September" from *One World at a Time,* by Ted Kooser, © 1985. Reprinted by permission of the University of Pittsburgh Press.

"Étude," "A Finding," "An Elegy," "Snakeskin," "A Letter in October," "A Heart of Gold," "Four Secretaries," "Shoes," "City Limits," "Site," "Surveyors," "Another Story," "Five-Finger Exercise," "Barn Owl," "Sparklers," "Old Dog in March," "The Great-Grandparents," and "Weather Central" from *Weather Central,* by Ted Kooser, © 1994. Reprinted by permission of the University of Pittsburgh Press.

It is out of the dailiness of life that one is
driven into the deepest recesses of the self.

STANLEY KUNITZ

CONTENTS

from Sure Signs
1980

from One World at a Time
1985

from The Blizzard Voices

1986

from Weather Central

1994

from Winter Morning Walks:
One Hundred Postcards to Jim Harrison

2000

from Delights & Shadows

2004

from Valentines

2008

from Splitting an Order

2014

from At Home

2017

New Poems

1

2

KINDEST REGARDS

from Sure Signs

1980

Selecting a Reader

First, I would have her be beautiful,
and walking carefully up on my poetry
at the loneliest moment of an afternoon,
her hair still damp at the neck
from washing it. She should be wearing
a raincoat, an old one, dirty
from not having money enough for the cleaners.
She will take out her glasses, and there
in the bookstore, she will thumb
over my poems, then put the book back
up on its shelf. She will say to herself,
"For that kind of money, I can get
my raincoat cleaned." And she will.

First Snow

The old black dog comes in one evening
with the first few snowflakes on his back
and falls asleep, throwing his bad leg out
at our excitement. This is the night
when one of us gets to say, as if it were news,
that no two snowflakes are ever alike;
the night when each of us remembers something
snowier. The kitchen is a kindergarten
steamy with stories. The dog gets stiffly up
and limps away, seeking a quiet spot
at the heart of the house. Outside,
in silence, with diamonds in his fur,
the winter night curls round the legs of the trees,
sleepily blinking snowflakes from his lashes.

An Old Photograph

This old couple, Nils and Lydia,
were married for seventy years.
Here they are sixty years old
and already like brother
and sister—small, lusterless eyes,
large ears, the same serious line
to the mouths. After those years
spent together, sharing
the weather of sex, the sour milk
of lost children, barns burning,
grasshoppers, fevers and silence,
they were beginning to share
their hard looks. How far apart
they sit; not touching at shoulder
or knee, hands clasped in their laps
as if under each pair was a key
to a trunk hidden somewhere,
full of those lessons one keeps
to oneself.
       They had probably
risen at daybreak, and dressed
by the stove, Lydia wearing
black wool with a collar of lace,
Nils his worn suit. They had driven
to town in the wagon and climbed
to the studio only to make
this stern statement, now veined
like a leaf, that though they looked
just alike they were separate people,

with separate wishes already
gone stale, a good two feet of space
between them, thirty years to go.

The Constellation Orion

I'm delighted to see you,
old friend,
lying there in your hammock
over the next town.
You were the first person
my son was to meet in the heavens.
He's sleeping now,
his head like a small sun in my lap.
Our car whizzes along in the night.
If he were awake, he'd say,
"Look, Daddy, there's Old Ryan!"
but I won't wake him.
He's mine for the weekend,
Old Ryan, not yours.

The Salesman

Today he's wearing his vinyl shoes,
shiny and white as little Karmann Ghias
fresh from the body shop, and as he moves
in his door-to-door glide, these shoes fly round
each other, honking the horns of their soles.
His hose are black and ribbed and tight, as thin
as an old umbrella or the wing of a bat.
(They leave a pucker when he pulls them off.)
He's got on his double-knit leisure suit
in a pond-scum green, with a tight white belt
that matches his shoes but suffers with cracks
at the golden buckle. His shirt is brown
and green, like a pile of leaves, and it opens
onto the neck at a Brillo pad
of graying hair which tosses a cross and chain
as he walks. The collar is splayed out over
the jacket's lapels yet leaves a lodge pin
taking the sun like a silver spike.
He's swinging a briefcase full of the things
of this world, a leather cornucopia
heavy with promise. Through those dark lenses,
each of the doors along your sunny street
looks slightly ajar, and in your quiet house
the dog of your willpower cowers and growls,
then crawls in under the basement steps,
making the jingle of coin with its tags.

Old Soldiers' Home

On benches in front of the Old Soldiers' Home,
the old soldiers unwrap the pale brown packages
of their hands, folding the fingers back
and looking inside, then closing them up again
and gazing off across the grounds,
safe with the secret.

Fort Robinson

When I visited Fort Robinson,
where Dull Knife and his Northern Cheyenne
were held captive that terrible winter,
the grounds crew was killing the magpies.

Two men were going from tree to tree
with sticks and ladders, poking the young birds
down from their nests and beating them to death
as they hopped about in the grass.

Under each tree where the men had worked
were twisted knots of clotted feathers,
and above each tree a magpie circled,
crazily calling in all her voices.

We didn't get out of the car.
My little boy hid in the back and cried
as we drove away, into those ragged buttes
the Cheyenne climbed that winter, fleeing.

How to Foretell a Change in the Weather

Rain always follows the cattle
sniffing the air and huddling
in fields with their heads to the lee.
You will know that the weather is changing
when your sheep leave the pasture
too slowly, and your dogs lie about
and look tired; when the cat
turns her back to the fire,
washing her face, and the pigs
wallow in litter; cocks will be crowing
at unusual hours, flapping their wings;
hens will chant; when your ducks
and your geese are too noisy,
and the pigeons are washing themselves;
when the peacocks squall loudly
from the tops of the trees,
when the guinea fowl grate;
when sparrows chip loudly
and fuss in the roadway, and when swallows
fly low, skimming the earth;
when the carrion crow
croaks to himself, and wild fowl
dip and wash, and when moles
throw up hills with great fervor;
when toads creep out in numbers;
when frogs croak; when bats
enter the houses; when birds
begin to seek shelter,
and the robin approaches your house;
when the swan flies at the wind,

and your bees leave the hive;
when ants carry their eggs to and fro,
and flies bite, and the earthworm
is seen on the surface of things.

Snow Fence

The red fence
takes the cold trail
north; no meat
on its ribs,
but neither has it
much to carry.

In an Old Apple Orchard

The wind's an old man
to this orchard; these trees
have been feeling
the soft tug of his gloves
for a hundred years.
Now it's April again,
and again that old fool
thinks he's young.
He's combed the dead leaves
out of his beard; he's put on
perfume. He's gone off
late in the day
toward the town, and come back
slow in the morning,
reeling with bees.
As late as noon, if you look
in the long grass,
you can see him
still rolling about in his sleep.

After the Funeral:
Cleaning Out the Medicine Cabinet

Behind this mirror no new world
opens to Alice. Instead, we find
the old world, rearranged in rows,
a dusty little chronicle
of small complaints and private sorrows,
each cough caught dry and airless
in amber, the sore feet powdered
and cool in their yellow can.
To this world turned the burning eyes
after their search, the weary back
after its lifting, the heavy heart
like an old dog, sniffing the lids
for an answer. Now one of us
unscrews the caps and tries the air
of each disease. Another puts
the booty in a shoe box: tins
of laxatives and aspirin,
the corn pads and the razor blades,
while still another takes the vials
of secret sorrows—the little pills
with faded, lonely codes—holding
them out the way one holds a spider
pinched in a tissue, and pours them down
the churning toilet and away.

Carrie

"There's never an end to dust
and dusting," my aunt would say
as her rag, like a thunderhead,
scudded across the yellow oak
of her little house. There she lived
seventy years with a ball
of compulsion closed in her fist,
and an elbow that creaked and popped
like a branch in a storm. Now dust
is her hands and dust her heart.
There's never an end to it.

For a Friend

Late November, driving to Wichita.
A black veil of starlings
snags on a thicket and falls.
Shadows of wings skitter over
the highway, like leaves, like ashes.

You have been dead for six months;
though summer and fall
were lighter by one life,
they didn't seem to show it.
The seasons, those steady horses,
are used to the fickle weight
of our shifting load.

I'll guess how it was; on the road
through the wood, you stood up
in the back of the hangman's cart,
reached a low-hanging branch,
and swung up into the green leaves
of our memories.
                            Old friend,
the stars were shattered windowglass
for weeks; we all were sorry.

They never found that part of you
that made you drink, that made you cruel.
You knew we loved you anyway.

Black streak across the centerline,
all highways make me think of you.

Five P.M.

The pigeon flies to her resting place
on a window ledge above the traffic,
and her shadow, which cannot fly, climbs
swiftly over the bricks to meet her there.

Just so are you and I gathered at 5:00,
your bicycle left by the porch, the wind
still ringing in it, and my shoes by the bed,
still warm from walking home to you.

Abandoned Farmhouse

He was a big man, says the size of his shoes
on a pile of broken dishes by the house;
a tall man, too, says the length of the bed
in an upstairs room; and a good, God-fearing man,
says the Bible with a broken back
on the floor below the window, dusty with sun;
but not a man for farming, say the fields
cluttered with boulders and the leaky barn.

A woman lived with him, says the bedroom wall
papered with lilacs and the kitchen shelves
covered with oilcloth, and they had a child,
says the sandbox made from a tractor tire.
Money was scarce, say the jars of plum preserves
and canned tomatoes sealed in the cellar hole.
And the winters cold, say the rags in the window frames.
It was lonely here, says the narrow country road.

Something went wrong, says the empty house
in the weed-choked yard. Stones in the field
say he was not a farmer; the still-sealed jars
in the cellar say she left in a nervous haste.
And the child? Its toys are strewn in the yard
like branches after a storm—a rubber cow,
a rusty tractor with a broken plow,
a doll in overalls. Something went wrong, they say.

At the Bait Stand

Part barn, part boxcar, part of a chicken shed,
part leaking water, something partly dead,
part pop machine, part gas pump, part a chair
leaned back against the wall, and sleeping there,
part-owner Herman Runner, mostly fat,
hip-waders, undershirt, tattoos, and hat.

The Widow Lester

I was too old to be married,
but nobody told me,
I guess they didn't care enough.
How it had hurt, though, catching bouquets
all those years!
Then I met Ivan, and kept him,
and never knew love.
How his feet stank in the bedsheets!
I could have told him to wash,
but I wanted to hold that stink against him.
The day he dropped dead in the field,
I was watching.
I was hanging up sheets in the yard,
and I finished.

The Red Wing Church

There's a tractor in the doorway of a church
in Red Wing, Nebraska, in a coat of mud
and straw that drags the floor. A broken plow
sprawls beggar-like behind it on some planks
that make a sort of roadway up the steps.
The steeple's gone. A black tar-paper scar
that lightning might have made replaces it.
They've taken it down to change the house of God
to Homer Johnson's barn, but it's still a church,
with clumps of tiger lilies in the grass
and one of those boxlike, glassed-in signs
that give the sermon's topic (reading now
a birdnest and a little broken glass).
The good works of the Lord are all around:
the steeple top is standing in a garden
just up the alley; it's a henhouse now:
fat leghorns gossip at its crowded door.
Pews stretch on porches up and down the street,
the stained-glass windows style the mayor's house,
and the bell's atop the firehouse in the square.
The cross is only God knows where.

from One World at a Time

1985

Flying at Night

Above us, stars. Beneath us, constellations.
Five billion miles away, a galaxy dies
like a snowflake falling on water. Below us,
some farmer, feeling the chill of that distant death,
snaps on his yard light, drawing his sheds and barn
back into the little system of his care.
All night, the cities, like shimmering novas,
tug with bright streets at lonely lights like his.

In the Basement of the Goodwill Store

In musty light, in the thin brown air
of damp carpet, doll heads, and rust,
beneath long rows of sharp footfalls
like nails in a lid, an old man stands
trying on glasses, lifting each pair
from the box like a glittering fish
and holding it up to the light
of a dirty bulb. Near him, a heap
of enameled pans as white as skulls
looms in the catacomb shadows,
and old toilets with dry red throats
cough up bouquets of curtain rods.

You've seen him somewhere before.
He's wearing the green leisure suit
you threw out with the garbage,
and the Christmas tie you hated,
and the ventilated wingtip shoes
you found in your father's closet
and wore as a joke. And the glasses
that finally fit him, through which
he looks to see you looking back—
two mirrors that flash and glance—
are those through which one day
you too will look down over the years,
when you have grown old and thin
and no longer particular,
and the things you once thought
you were rid of forever
have taken you back in their arms.

In January, 1962

With his hat on the table before him,
my grandfather waited until it was time
to go to my grandmother's funeral.
Beyond the window, his eighty-eighth winter
lay white in its furrows. The little creek
that cut through his cornfield was frozen.
Past the creek and the broken, brown stubble,
on a hill that thirty years before
he'd given the town, a green tent flapped
under the cedars. Throughout the day before,
he'd stayed there by the window watching
the blue woodsmoke from the thawing-barrels
catch in the bitter wind and vanish,
and had seen, so small in the distance,
a man breaking the earth with a pick.
I suppose he could feel that faraway work
in his hands—the steel-smooth, cold oak handle;
the thick, dull shock at the wrists—
for the following morning, as we waited there,
it was as if it hurt him to move them,
those hard old hands that lay curled and still
near the soft gray felt hat on the table.

Father

Theodore Briggs Kooser
May 19, 1902–December 31, 1979

You spent fifty-five years
walking the hard floors
of the retail business:
first, as a boy playing store

in your grandmother's barn,
sewing feathers on hats
the neighbors had thrown out,
then stepping out onto

the smooth pine planks
of your uncle's grocery—
SALADA TEA in gold leaf
over the door, your uncle

and father still young then
in handlebar mustaches,
white aprons with dusters
tucked into their sashes—

then to the varnished oak
of a dry goods store—
music to your ears,
that bumpety-bump

of bolts of bright cloth
on the counter tops,

the small rattle of buttons,
the bell in the register—

then on to the cold tile
of a bigger store, and then one
still bigger—gray carpet,
wide aisles, a new town

to get used to—then into
retirement, a few sales
in your own garage,
the concrete under your feet.

You had good legs, Dad,
and a good storekeeper's eye:
asked once if you remembered
a teacher of mine,

you said, "I certainly do;
size 10, a little something
in blue." How you loved
what you'd done with your life!

Now you're gone, and the clerks
are lazy, the glass cases
smudged, the sale sweaters
pulled off on the floor.

But what good times we had
before it was over:
after those stores had closed,
you posing as customers,

strutting in big, flowered hats,
those aisles like a stage,
the pale mannequins watching;
we laughed till we cried.

The Fan in the Window

It is September, and a cool breeze
from somewhere ahead is turning the blades;
night, and the slow flash of the fan
the last light between us and the darkness.
Dust has begun to collect on the blades,
haymaker's dust from distant fields,
dust riding to town on the night-black wings
of the crows, a thin frost of dust
that clings to the fan in just the way
we cling to the earth as it spins.
The fan has brought us through,
its shiny blades like the screw of a ship
that has pushed its way through summer—
cut flowers awash in its wake,
the stagnant Sargasso Sea of July
far behind us. For the moment, we rest,
we lie in the dark hull of the house,
we rock in the troughs off the shore
of October, the engine cooling,
the fan blades so lazily turning, but turning.

Daddy Longlegs

Here, on fine long legs springy as steel,
a life rides, sealed in a small brown pill
that skims along over the basement floor
wrapped up in a simple obsession.
Eight legs reach out like the master ribs
of a web in which some thought is caught
dead center in its own small world,
a thought so far from the touch of things
that we can only guess at it. If mine,
it would be the secret dream
of walking alone across the floor of my life
with an easy grace, and with love enough
to live on at the center of myself.

Goodbye

You lean with one arm out
against the porch post,
your big hand cupping its curve,
shy of that handshake
we both know is coming.
And when we've said enough,
when the last small promises
begin to repeat, your eyes
come to mine, and then
you offer your hand,
dusted with chalk from the post,
and sticky with parting.

Laundry

A pink house trailer,
scuffed and rusted, sunken
in weeds. On the line,

five pale blue workshirts
up to their elbows
in raspberry canes—

a good, clean crew
of pickers, out early,
sleeves wet with dew,

and near them, a pair
of bright yellow panties
urging them on.

Ladder

Against the low roof of a house
in the suburbs, someone has left
a ladder leaning, an old wooden ladder
too heavy to take down for the night
and put up in the morning, the kind
that reaches beyond such a roof
by a good six feet, punching up
into the sky. The kind with paint
from another world on its rungs,
the cream- and butter-colored spots
from another time, the kind that
before you get up in the morning
knocks hard at the front of your house
like a sheriff, that stands there
in front of your door with a smile;
a ladder with solid authority,
with its pantlegs pressed, a ladder
that if it could whistle would whistle.

Walking at Noon near the Burlington Depot in Lincoln, Nebraska

To the memory of James Wright

On the rat-gray dock
of the candy factory,
workers in caps and aprons
as white as divinity
sit on their heels and smoke
in the warm spring sunlight
thick with butterscotch.

In the next block down,
outside a warehouse,
its big doors rolled and bolted
over the dusty hush
of pyramids of cartons,
two pickets in lettered vests
call back and forth, their voices
a clatter of echoes.

A girl sits in her car,
an old tan Oldsmobile
broken down over its tires,
and plays the radio.

On the grille of a semi
smelling of heat and distance,
one tattered butterfly.

And an empty grocery cart
from Safeway, miles from here,
leans into its reflection
in a blackened window, a little
piano recital of chrome
for someone to whom all things
were full of sadness.

At Nightfall

In feathers the color of dusk, a swallow,
up under the shadowy eaves of the barn,
weaves now, with skillful beak and chitter,
one bright white feather into her nest
to guide her flight home in the darkness.
It has taken a hundred thousand years
for a bird to learn this one trick with a feather,
a simple thing. And the world is alive
with such innocent progress. But to what
safe place shall any of us return
in the last smoky nightfall,
when we in our madness have put the torch
to the hope in every nest and feather?

Cleaning a Bass

She put it on the chopping block
and it flopped a little, the red rickrack
of its sharp gills sawing the evening air
into lengths, its yellow eyes like glass,
like the eyes of a long-forgotten doll
in the light of an attic. "They feel no pain,"
she told me, setting the fish upright,
and with a chunk of stovewood
she drove an ice pick through its skull
and into the block. The big fish curled
on its pin like a silver pennant
and then relaxed, but I could see life
in those eyes, which stared at the darkening
world of the air with a terrible wonder.
"It's true," she said, looking over at me
through the gathering shadows, "they feel no pain,"
and she took her Swedish filleting knife
with its beautiful blade that leaped and flashed
like a fish itself, and with one stroke
laid the bass bare to its shivering spine.

A Letter

I have tried a dozen ways
to say these things
and have failed: how the moon
with its bruises
climbs branch over branch
through the empty tree;
how the cool November dusk,
like a wind, has blown
these old gray houses up
against the darkness;
and what these things
have come to mean to me
without you. I raked the yard
this morning, and it rained
this afternoon. Tonight,
along the shiny street,
the bags of leaves—
wet-shouldered
but warm in their skins—
are huddled together, close,
so close to life.

The *Voyager 2* Satellite

The tin man is cold;
the glitter of distant worlds
is like snow on his coat.
Free-falling through space,
he spreads his arms
and slowly turns,
hands reaching to catch
the white, elusive
dandelion fuzz
of starlight. He is the dove
with wings of purest gold
sent out upon the deep
to seek a place for us,
the goat upon whose back
we've sent our problems
into exile, the dreamy beast
of peace and silence
who now grows smaller, smaller,
falling so gracefully
into the great blank face
of God.

As the President Spoke

As the President spoke, he raised a finger
to emphasize something he said. I've forgotten
just what he was saying, but as he spoke
he glanced at that finger as if it were
somebody else's, and his face went slack and gray,
and he folded his finger back into his hand
and put it down under the podium
along with whatever it meant, with whatever he'd seen
as it spun out and away from that bony axis.

The Urine Specimen

In the clinic, a sun-bleached shell of stone
on the shore of the city, you enter
the last small chamber, a little closet
chastened with pearl—cool, white, and glistening—
and over the chilly well of the toilet
you trickle your precious sum in a cup.
It's as simple as that. But the heat
of this gold your body's melted and poured out
into a form begins to enthrall you,
warming your hand with your flesh's fevers
in a terrible way. It's like holding
an organ—spleen or fatty pancreas,
a lobe from your foamy brain still steaming
with worry. You know that just outside
a nurse is waiting to cool it into a gel
and slice it onto a microscope slide
for the doctor, who in it will read your future,
wringing his hands. You lift the chalice and toast
the long life of your friend there in the mirror,
who wanly smiles, but does not drink to you.

Porch Swing in September

The porch swing hangs fixed in a morning sun
that bleaches its gray slats, its flowered cushion
whose flowers have faded, like those of summer,
and a small brown spider has hung out her web
on a line between porch post and chain
so that no one may swing without breaking it.
She is saying it's time that the swinging were done with,
time that the creaking and pinging and popping
that sang through the ceiling were past,
time now for the soft vibrations of moths,
the wasp tapping each board for an entrance,
the cool dewdrops to brush from her work
every morning, one world at a time.

from The Blizzard Voices

1986

A Woman's Voice

Eighteen eighty-eight, a Thursday,
the twelfth of January:
It had been warm all morning,
with a soft, southerly breeze
melting the snowdrifts back
from the roads. There were bobwhite
and prairie chickens out
pecking for grit in the wheel-ruts.
On lines near shacks and soddies,
women were airing their bedding—
bright quilts that flapped and billowed,
ticks sodden as thunderheads.
In the muddy schoolyards, children
were rolling the wet gray snow
into men, into fortresses,
laughing and splashing about
in their shirtsleeves. Their teachers
stood in the doorways and watched.

Odd weather for January;
a low line of clouds in the north;
too warm, too easy. And the air
filled with electricity;
an iron poker held up
close to a stovepipe would spark,
and a comb drawn through the hair
would crackle. One woman said
she'd had to use a stick of wood
to open her oven door.

A Man's Voice

Father and I had pulled the pump up
out of the well to put
new leathers in the cylinders.
I looked toward the house and saw
that our cats were spinning around
and around on the steps
as if they were drunk. Then the air
was suddenly full of snow,
weeds, dust and fodder, blowing
out of the northwest. We ran in
and pulled the door shut, snapping
the bottom hinge in the wind.
A wall of snow hit the house
and shook it hard, and it grew dark
as night. We had plenty of coal
to burn, as Father had bought a load
the week before. Through the night,
the house rocked like a cradle,
cracking much of the plaster loose.
In the morning we found
the wind had packed the snow so hard
our horses could walk on it
without breaking the crust.
The drifts were there till June.

A Woman's Voice

My maiden name was Hanna,
and I was twelve at the time.
We had been playing Fox-and-Geese
in the schoolyard, during
the afternoon recess,
when the blizzard bore down
out of the northwest, roaring
and whistling, loud as a train.
There was lightning in front,
and it looked like bales of cotton
twenty-five feet high, tied up
with flashing silver wire.
I shall never forget that night,
as we stood close by the stove
in that creaking, drafty schoolhouse,
doing our best to comfort
the little ones, who were cold
and afraid of the darkness.
We sang all the songs we knew,
including "Blow winter winds,
as hard as you will; we shall
be gay and happy still."

A Man's Voice

Depending where on the plains
you were that day, there was between
eight inches and a foot of snow
fresh on the ground. From all accounts,
the blizzard picked it up
and ground it fine to a powder,
then added another foot
of new snow to it. The drifts
on the morning after the storm
were twenty and thirty feet deep.
In one low draw, a windmill
thirty-five feet high was covered
clear up to the topmost blades.
Houses and barns were buried,
and one man found his soddy
by falling in through the roof.
The temperature dropped
from just above freezing, at three,
to fifty below the next morning.

A Woman's Voice

I was an Ohio girl
who taught in a country school.
How I remember that day!
When the blizzard hit, it blew
some of the shutters closed
with a bang, breaking some panes,
and the snow came pouring in.
Toward evening, our fuel was gone,
so we set out walking,
holding one another's hands.
It was impossible to see,
but we followed a row
of dead sunflower stalks
all the way to a nearby farm.
I never see a sunflower now
that I don't count my lucky stars.

A Man's Voice

Corn was at twelve cents a bushel,
a good deal cheaper than coal,
so we fed our stoves with corn
and, sometimes, with twists of hay
or cowchips. Some folks had
the new Hay-Burner stoves
that would burn all night on one twist,
but not us. On the night
that the big storm struck, we burned
the floorboards from the side-porch
and some of the furniture
because we couldn't reach the barn
for fuel. My sister was born
about two in the morning
with my grandmother tending
my mother. We pinned up quilts
and sheets along the walls
and over the bed to keep the snow
off Mother and the baby.

A Woman's Voice

In all my years I never saw
another thing like that storm.
When it came it felt as if
an enormous fist had struck
the house. Snow fine as flour
sifted in under the eaves
and piled along the walls.
Our youngest, Jim, was at school
on a place two miles above,
and we were worried sick
for fear he'd try to get home
and be lost. You couldn't see
your hand at the end of your arm
out in it. My husband led
one of the horses up the lane
but had to turn back. The snow
had frozen the horse's eyes.
Halvor was just drying out
by the stove when we heard
a knocking out on the porch,
and there stood Jimmy's pony,
covered with ice and snow,
with a bag on her halter,
and in it a note which said
"Your boy is safe at the school."

A Man's Voice

So go the old stories,
like wind in the long grass,
loose wind singing in fences,
wind like the white wolf
moving in over the snow.
Nobody knows now
how many died; some say
two hundred or more
in Dakota Territory,
Nebraska, and Kansas.
Few records were kept;
the dead were buried at home,
in poorly marked graves
in the corners of fields.
All that was long ago,
but the wind in the hedgerow,
the wind lifting the dust
in the empty schools,
the wind which in the tin fan
of the windmill catches,
turning the wheel to the north—
that wind remembers their names.

from Weather Central

1994

Étude

I have been watching a Great Blue Heron
fish in the cattails, easing ahead
with the stealth of a lover composing a letter,
the hungry words looping and blue
as they coil and uncoil, as they kiss and sting.

Let's say that he holds down an everyday job
in an office. His blue suit blends in.
Long days swim beneath the glass top
of his desk, each one alike. On the lip
of each morning, a bubble trembles.

No one has seen him there, writing a letter
to a woman he loves. His pencil is poised
in the air like the beak of a bird.
He would spear the whole world if he could,
toss it and swallow it live.

A Finding

One of my dogs has brought the foreleg of a deer
up from the bottom woods, and gnawed on it awhile,
and left it next to the door like a long-stemmed rose,
the joint at its shoulder red and flowering
where the dog has neatly licked the earth away.

Often they die like that, gut-shot by a hunter
or carrying an arrow for miles. I've found their bones
up under banks where they've hidden in caves of roots,
curled themselves over their pain, and kicked at the coyotes.
And the dogs have found far more of them than I.

Picking it up, a delicate life runs lightly
over my hands. The knee-joint's smooth articulation
folds the leg into itself like a carpenter's rule.
There's a spring to these bones, the hair laid back from flying,
the hoof like a castanet ready to clatter.

The wind lifts just a little, gets in under the fur,
and I see on the shin a tiny, tar black scar
from a barbed-wire fence leapt not so long ago.
My two dogs stand and look out over the fields,
and the three of us can hear that wire still thrumming.

An Elegy

In summer, after the spring floods
have fallen away, there are always
the thin, girlish leaves of the willows
left by the river to dry—
draped over tangles of driftwood,
thrown over the roots of old trees—
their greenness gone, their ribs and webbing
spun into a thick, dull paper
upon which all the words have run together,
whatever they said. But you must know
that the field mouse now finds shelter there,
and the leopard frog who sings all night,
and the water strider setting out
across the water, long-legged and light
as a breath.

Snakeskin

It is only the old yellow shell
of something long gone on,
a dusty tunnel echoing
with light, yet you can feel
the speed along it, feel
in your bones the tick of wheels.

You hold a glove of lace,
a loose glitter of sequins.
The ghost of a wind is in it still
for someone only yesterday
was waving it: goodbye.

Somewhere, a long train
crosses a border. The sun lights lamps
in its thousand round windows.
All it knows is behind it already.
Nothing it knows is ahead.
Its whistle flicks into the distance.

A Letter in October

Dawn comes later and later now,
and I, who only a month ago
could sit with coffee every morning
watching the light walk down the hill
to the edge of the pond and place
a doe there, shyly drinking,

then see the light step out upon
the water, sowing reflections
to either side—a garden
of trees that grew as if by magic—
now see no more than my face,
mirrored by darkness, pale and odd,

startled by time. While I slept,
night in its thick winter jacket
bridled the doe with a twist
of wet leaves and led her away,
then brought its black horse with harness
that creaked like a cricket, and turned

the water garden under. I woke,
and at the waiting window found
the curtains open to my open face;
beyond me, darkness. And I,
who only wished to keep looking out,
must now keep looking in.

Four Secretaries

All through the day I hear or overhear
their clear, light voices calling
from desk to desk, young women whose fingers
play casually over their documents,

setting the incoming checks to one side,
the thick computer reports to the other,
tapping the correspondence into stacks
while they sing to each other, not intending

to sing nor knowing how beautiful
their voices are as they call back and forth,
singing their troubled marriage ballads,
their day-care, car-park, landlord songs.

Even their anger with one another
is lovely: the color rising in their throats,
their white fists clenched in their laps,
the quiet between them that follows.

And their sadness—how deep and full of love
is their sadness when one among them
is hurt, and they hear her calling
and gather about her to cry.

Shoes

In the shoe store storage closet,
the smooth brown eggs of new shoes
lie glowing in boxes, nestled
in christening gowns, their eyelets
already open and staring
but their laces still tightly folded
in dark little fists. Let us
not tell them just yet
that they will all too soon
be just like the others, waiting in rank
by size and sex and color
at the secondhand store—
old shoes with cracked faces,
with sore hands fanned out on their knees,
their toes turned up from forever
walking uphill in the rain.

City Limits

Here on the west edge, the town turned its back on the west,
gave up the promise, nodded goodbye to a highway
that narrowed away, and with a sunset-red bandanna
bid the shimmering tracks go on, go on.

Go west, young man, cheered Horace Greeley, and west
rattled the new country, rocking along through the sparks,
the cattle dying, the children sick, the limits
always ahead like a wall of black mountains.

But the steam cooled and condensed, the pistons rusted.
The dead weight of trunks thudded onto the platform,
bursting their leather straps. Generations spilled out
and we settled for limits: strung fence wire, drew plat maps

with streets squared to the polestar, passed finicky laws,
built churches true: the bubble centered in the spirit level.
We let the plumb bob swing till it stopped with its point
on the spot where we were, where we were to remain.

The frontier rolled on ahead; we never caught up
with whatever it was, that rolling wave or weather front,
those wings of cloud. The news came back, delivered by failure,
a peach-crate of rags, a face caved in over its smiles.

We thrived on the failure of others; rich gossip
flowered like vines on the trellises. On porches,
what once had been dream leaned back on its rockers.
We could have told them. We could have told them so.

The bean-strings ran back and forth through the vines
defining our limits. Children played by the rules:
cat's cradle, Red Rover. Morticians showed up
with wagons of markers. The dead lay in their places.

Our horses grew heavy and lame tied to pickets
and our wheel-rims rusted and sprang from their spokes.
Fire-pit became city, its flashing red pennants strung
over the car lot. We signed on the line at the bank.

What we'd done to the Indians happened to us.
Our hearts had never been in it, this stopping;
we wanted a nowhere but gave ourselves over to gardens.
Now our old campsite limits itself on the west

to the lazy abandon of sunset—a pint bottle
whistling the blues in a dry prairie wind. Next to
the tracks, turning first one way and then another,
a switch with red eyes wipes its mouth with a sleeve.

Site

A fenced-in square of sand and yellow grass,
five miles or more from the nearest town,
is the site where the County Poor Farm stood
for seventy years, and here the County
permitted the poor to garden, permitted them
use of the County water from a hand-pump,
lent them buckets to carry it spilling
over the grass to the sandy, burning furrows
that drank it away—a kind of Workfare
from 1900. At night, each family slept
on the floor of one room in a boxy house
that the County put up and permitted them
use of. It stood here somewhere, door
facing the road. And somewhere under this grass
lie the dead in the County's unmarked graves,
each body buried with a mason jar in which
each person's name is written on a paper.
The County provided the paper and the jars.

Surveyors

They have come from the past,
wearing their orange doublets
like medieval pages.

Seeing through time, they see
nothing of us. For them
the world is rock upon rock.

There is always the one
on one side of the highway,
holding his yellow staff,

and one on the other,
his one eye boring through
cars and trucks. It is as if

we were all invisible,
streaming between them
like ghosts, not snapping

the tightened string of light
they hold between them, nor
catching it across the bumper

and dragging them bouncing
behind us into our lives.
We mean nothing to them

in our waxed sedans, in our
business suits and fresh spring
dresses. They stand by the road

in the leaning grass, lifting
their heavy gloves of gold
to wave across the traffic,

and though they cannot see us,
helpfully we wave back.

Another Story

In a country churchyard, two workmen
were digging a grave. It was summer,
but cool in the cedar-blue shade
of the white clapboard church where they labored.

Their picks did all of the talking.
Beyond them, a field of tall corn
glittered with heat, and above, a lone bird
rose on the air like an ash.

The grave grew slowly down
and out of the world, and the world rolled
under the work. Then the men stopped.
One stooped to scrape in the clay.

When he stood, light-headed,
swaying a little, he held in his hand
an old cowbell, covered with dirt
and packed with darkness.

He scraped out the earth with his knife.
The bell had no clapper. He shook it.
A meadowlark piped on a fence post.
In the distance, a feeder thunked.

He handed it across the grave
to the younger man, who held it in his hands
like a baby bird, then rang it tenderly.
A crow cawed in a cedar top.

He rang it again. On the highway,
a mile away, a semi trumpeted.
In the cornfield, an irrigation pump
thumped with a regular heartbeat.

He handed it back to the older man,
who set it aside. All afternoon,
they worked without a word between them.
At intervals each touched the empty bell.

Five-Finger Exercise

All day at home, alone in the winter half-light,
I watched the wild birds feeding, coming and going,
their flight light as ashes over the yellow coals
of cracked corn, of millet and linnet seed.
And because of a darkness feeding in me, I saw
in bare branches the rags of a frock coat flying,
the charred pages of hymnals settling through smoke,
candle wax cooling, becoming the breast of a sparrow.
And as I waited there, five small blackbirds as quick
as quarter notes touched down at once, striking
a perfect chord at the cold, high end of the keyboard,
and it frightened them, and off they flew together.

Sparklers

I scratched your name in longhand
on the night, then you wrote mine.
I couldn't see you, near me,
laughing and chasing my name
through the air, but I think
I could hear your heart, and feel your breath
against the darkness, hurrying.

One word swirled out of your hand
as you rushed hard to write it
all the way out to its end
before its beginning was gone.
It left a frail red line
trembling along on the darkness,
and that was my name.

Old Dog in March

From a cold stone stoop,
stepping down slowly
into another spring,

stretching his back,
stretching his back legs,
one leg at a time,

making a bridge
with his spine, reaching
from winter out and out,

forever out it seems,
then quaking at the end of it,
all down his length

so that his claws
skitter a little, losing
their grip on the world,

an old brown dog
gone stiff from chasing
all winter through dreams,

recovers his balance,
and, one ache at a time,
lowers himself

to the solid field of promise,
where with pink tip
of tongue between his teeth,

and frosty muzzle,
he sips the cool, delicious,
richly storied wind.

The Great-Grandparents

As small children, we were taken to meet them.
They had recently arrived from another world
and stood dumbfounded in the busy depot
of the present, their useless belongings in piles:
old tools, old words, old recipes, secrets.
They searched our faces and grasped our hands
as if we could lead them back, but we drew them
forward into the future, feeling them tremble,
their shirt cuffs yellow, smoky old woodstoves
smoldering somewhere under their clothes.

Weather Central

Each evening at six fifteen, the weatherman
turns a shoulder to us, extends his hand,
and talking softly as a groom, cautiously
smooths and strokes the massive, dappled flank
of the continent, touching the cloudy whorls
that drift like galaxies across its hide,
tracing the loops of harness with their barbs
and bells and pennants; then, with a horsefly's touch,
he brushes a mountain range and sets a shudder
running just under the skin. His bearing
is cavalier from years of success and he laughs
at the science, yet makes no sudden moves
that might startle that splendid order
or loosen the physics. One would not want to wake
the enormous Appaloosa mare of weather,
asleep in her stall on a peaceful moonlit night.

from Winter Morning Walks:
One Hundred Postcards
to Jim Harrison

2000

Epigraph

The quarry road tumbles toward me
out of the early morning darkness,
lustrous with frost, an unrolled bolt
of softly glowing fabric, interwoven
with tiny glass beads on silver thread,
the cloth spilled out and then lovingly
smoothed by my father's hand
as he stands behind his wooden counter
(dark as these fields) at Tilden's Store
so many years ago. "Here," he says smiling,
"you can make something special with this."

November 9

Rainy and cold.

The sky hangs thin and wet on its clothesline.

A deer of gray vapor steps through the foreground,
under the dripping, lichen-rusted trees.

Halfway across the next field,
the distance (or can that be the future?)
is sealed up in tin like an old barn.

November 10

High winds all night.

Most of the snow passed north of us,
but this morning we're given the fancy white lace
at the edge of that blanket,
every weed on the roadside coated with ice.

Behind the counter at the post office,
somebody's small carton stamped with block letters:
ANGEL MOMENTS WITH SNAIL.

I drive very slowly all the way home.

November 12

4:30 a.m.

On mornings like this, as hours before dawn
I walk the dark hall of the road
with my life creaking under my feet, I sometimes
take hold of the cold porcelain knob
of the moon, and turn it, and step into a room
warm and yellow, and take my seat
at a small wooden table with a border of painted pansies,
and wait for my mother to bring me my bowl.

November 18

Cloudy, dark, and windy.

Walking by flashlight
at six in the morning,
my circle of light on the gravel
swinging side to side,
coyote, raccoon, field mouse, sparrow,
each watching from darkness
this man with the moon on a leash.

November 29

Breezy and warm.

A round hay bale,
brown and blind, all shoulders,
huddled, bound tightly
in sky blue nylon twine.
Just so I awoke this morning,
wrapped in fear.

Oh, red plastic flag on a stick
stuck into loose gravel,
driven over, snapped off,
propped up again and again,
give me your courage.

December 2

Walking in darkness, in awe,
beneath a billion indifferent stars
at quarter to six in the morning,
the moon already down
and gone, but keeping a pale lamp burning
at the edge of the west,
my shoes too loud in the gravel
that, faintly lit, looks to be little more
than a contrail of vapor,
so thin, so insubstantial it could,
on a whim, let me drop through it
and out of the day,
but I have taught myself
to place one foot ahead of the other
in noisy confidence
as if each morning might be trusted,
as if the sounds I make might buoy me up.

December 14

Home from my walk, shoes off, at peace.

The weight of my old dog, Hattie—thirty-five pounds
of knocking bones, sighs, tremors and dreams—
just isn't enough to hold a patch of sun in its place,
at least for very long. While she shakes in her sleep,
it slips from beneath her and inches away,
taking the morning with it—the music from the radio,
the tea from my cup, the drowsy yellow hours—
picking up dust and dog hair as it goes.

December 20

Ten degrees at sunrise, light snow flying.

The beaver's mound of brush and cornstalks
stands at the edge of silence this morning,
a pyramid on an untracked desert of snow
with black, open water shining beyond it.
Somewhere inside are the hidden mysteries:
an old yellow-toothed pharaoh, wrapped up
in bandages of sleep, and on his shallow breath,
oily odor of tanbark and the priceless perfume
of summer willow leaves.

December 22

Five below zero.

The cold finds its way through the wall
by riding nails, common ten-penny nails
through a wall so packed with insulation
it wouldn't admit a single quarter-note
from the wind's soprano solo. Yet you can touch
this solid wall and feel the icy spots
where the nails have carried the outside
almost into the house, nickel-sized spots
like the frosty tips of fingers, groping,
and you can imagine the face
of the cold, all wreathed in flying hair,
its long fingers spread, its thin blue lips
pressed into the indifferent ear
of the siding, whispering something
not one of us inside can hear.

January 5

Eighteen degrees at sunrise.

Hung from the old loading chute
is a lasso of rusty wire,
and caught in the grain of its boards
is a wisp of red hair, and the heavy,
dead knocking of hooves.

January 7

Five degrees and light snow.

An elaborate braiding of deer tracks
close to the house this morning early,
within a few yards of our two dogs
asleep on the porch. A dozen or more
walking soundlessly east in the night,
a half-moon rising before them.
I like the long deft brushstroke
as each hoof swung into and out of the snow,
and the little splash kicked out ahead
as they stripped sweet bark from the darkness,
afraid of everything but not afraid.

January 12

Thirty-two degrees at sunrise.

You can catch an owl
that's been killing your chickens
by setting a trap on a post
in your poultry yard
and that's all I can call up
to describe that funeral tent
alive and wildly struggling
in a punishing wind
just thirty-seven years ago
this morning, and we mourners
huddled in the shadow
of those wings.

January 17

Dark and still at 5:30 a.m.

Some mornings, very early, I put on
my dead father's brown corduroy robe,
more than twenty years old, its lining torn,
the sleeves a little too long for me,
and walk through the house
with my father, groping our way
through the chilly, darkened rooms,
not wanting to waken our wives with a light,
and feeling on our outstretched fingers,
despite the familiar order of each room,
despite the warmth of women sleeping near,
the breath of emptiness.

January 19

Still thawing, breezy.

Arthritic and weak, my old dog Hattie
stumbles behind me over the snow.
When I stop, she stops, tipped to one side
like a folding table with one of the legs
not snapped in place. Head bowed, one ear
turned down to the earth as if she
could hear it turning, she is losing the trail
at the end of her fourteenth year.
Now she must follow. Once she could catch
a season running and shake it by the neck
till the leaves fell off, but now they get away,
flashing their tails as they bound off
over the hill. Maybe she doesn't see them
out of those clouded, wet brown eyes,
maybe she no longer cares. I thought
for a while last summer that I might die
before my dogs, but it seems I was wrong.
She wobbles a little way ahead of me now,
barking her sharp small bark,
then stops and trembles, excited, on point
at the spot that leads out of the world.

January 31

Light mist on a sharp wind.

Where two fences meet at a corner,
two thickets of bare plum bushes
also have met, and have blended
to soften the corner with clouds
of wine red canes and purple thorns.
Two weeks ago, they pulled a snowstorm
down out of the wind and spread
a long, soft drift beneath their branches,
and though by this morning the snow
had melted away from the field,
the drift sleeps, long and white and cold,
rounding the corner, an L shape
that gracefully tapers out to its ends
like a boomerang, a new one that never
flew back to the hand of the wind.

February 16

An early morning fog.

In fair weather, the shy past keeps its distance.
Old loves, old regrets, old humiliations
look on from afar. They stand back under the trees.
No one would think to look for them there.

But in fog they come closer. You can feel them
there by the road as you slowly walk past.
Still as fence posts they wait, dark and reproachful,
each stepping forward in turn.

February 18

Quiet and clear.

Dawn, and the snip-snip-snip of a chickadee
cutting a circle of light to line her nest.

March 2

Patchy clouds and windy.

All morning
our house has been flashing in and out of shade
like a signal, and far across the waves of grass
a neighbor's house has answered,
offering help. If I have to abandon this life,
they tell me they'll pull me across
in a leather harness
clipped to the telephone line.

March 7

Overcast, breezy and cold.

This morning I watched a red-tailed hawk,
wings back, drop like the head of a hatchet
into the ditch. Whatever she caught
in the deep dry grass, rabbit or mouse,
had a moment to lie there before it could die
while the hawk stretched to its full height,
fanned and then leisurely folded her wings,
tipped her head with a gleaming yellow eye
and for a minute watched it waiting.

March 12

5:30 a.m., dark and cold.

Only a crust of moon is left
to offer the morning,
but that may be enough for now,
what with our frosty picnic table
so heavily laden with stars.

March 20

The vernal equinox.

How important it must be
to someone
that I am alive, and walking,
and that I have written
these poems.
This morning the sun stood
right at the end of the road
and waited for me.

from Delights & Shadows

2004

Walking on Tiptoe

Long ago we quit lifting our heels
like the others—horse, dog, and tiger—
though we thrill to their speed
as they flee. Even the mouse
bearing the great weight of a nugget
of dog food is enviably graceful.
There is little spring to our walk,
we are so burdened with responsibility,
all of the disciplinary actions
that have fallen to us, the punishments,
the killings, and all with our feet
bound stiff in the skins of the conquered.
But sometimes, in the early hours,
we can feel what it must have been like
to be one of them, up on our toes,
stealing past doors where others are sleeping,
and suddenly able to see in the dark.

At the Cancer Clinic

She is being helped toward the open door
that leads to the examining rooms
by two young women I take to be her sisters.
Each bends to the weight of an arm
and steps with the straight, tough bearing
of courage. At what must seem to be
a great distance, a nurse holds the door,
smiling and calling encouragement.
How patient she is in the crisp white sails
of her clothes. The sick woman
peers from under her funny knit cap
to watch each foot swing scuffing forward
and take its turn under her weight.
There is no restlessness or impatience
or anger anywhere in sight. Grace
fills the clean mold of this moment
and all the shuffling magazines grow still.

Gyroscope

I place this within the first order
of wonders: a ten-year-old girl
alone on a sunny, glassed-in porch
in February, the world beyond
the windows slowly tipping forward
into spring, her thin arms held out
in the sleepwalker pose, and pinched
and stretched between her fingers,
a length of common grocery twine
upon which smoothly spins and leans
one of the smaller worlds we each
at one time learn to master, the last
to balance so lightly in our hands.

A Rainy Morning

A young woman in a wheelchair,
wearing a black nylon poncho spattered with rain,
is pushing herself through the morning.
You have seen how pianists
sometimes bend forward to strike the keys,
then lift their hands, draw back to rest,
then lean again to strike just as the chord fades.
Such is the way this woman
strikes at the wheels, then lifts her long white fingers,
letting them float, then bends again to strike
just as the chair slows, as if into a silence.
So expertly she plays the chords
of this difficult music she has mastered,
her wet face beautiful in its concentration,
while the wind turns the pages of rain.

Mourners

After the funeral, the mourners gather
under the rustling churchyard maples
and talk softly, like clusters of leaves.
White shirt cuffs and collars flash in the shade:
highlights on deep green water.
They came this afternoon to say goodbye,
but now they keep saying hello and hello,
peering into each other's faces,
slow to let go of each other's hands.

Skater

She was all in black but for a yellow ponytail
that trailed from her cap, and bright blue gloves
that she held out wide, the feathery fingers spread,
as surely she stepped, click-clack, onto the frozen
top of the world. And there, with a clatter of blades,
she began to braid a loose path that broadened
into a meadow of curls. Across the ice she swooped
and then turned back and, halfway, bent her legs
and leapt in the air the way a crane leaps, blue gloves
lifting her lightly, and turned a snappy half-turn
there in the wind before coming down, arms wide,
skating backward right out of that moment, smiling back
at the woman she'd been just an instant before.

Mother

Mid-April already, and the wild plums
bloom at the roadside, a lacy white
against the exuberant, jubilant green
of new grass and the dusty, fading black
of burned-out ditches. No leaves, not yet,
only the delicate, star-petaled
blossoms, sweet with their timeless perfume.

You have been gone a month today
and have missed three rains and one nightlong
watch for tornadoes. I sat in the cellar
from six to eight while fat spring clouds
went somersaulting, rumbling east. Then it poured,
a storm that walked on legs of lightning,
dragging its shaggy belly over the fields.

The meadowlarks are back, and the finches
are turning from green to gold. Those same
two geese have come to the pond again this year,
honking in over the trees and splashing down.
They never nest, but stay a week or two
then leave. The peonies are up, the red sprouts
burning in circles like birthday candles,

for this is the month of my birth, as you know,
the best month to be born in, thanks to you,
everything ready to burst with living.
There will be no more new flannel nightshirts
sewn on your old black Singer, no birthday card

addressed in a shaky but businesslike hand.
You asked me if I would be sad when it happened

and I am sad. But the iris I moved from your house
now hold in the dusty dry fists of their roots
green knives and forks as if waiting for dinner,
as if spring were a feast. I thank you for that.
Were it not for the way you taught me to look
at the world, to see the life at play in everything,
I would have to be lonely forever.

A Jar of Buttons

This is a core sample
from the floor of the Sea of Mending,

a cylinder packed with shells
that over many years

sank through fathoms of shirts—
pearl buttons, blue buttons—

and settled together
beneath waves of perseverance,

an ocean upon which
generations of women set forth,

under the sails of gingham curtains,
and, seated side by side

on decks sometimes salted by tears,
made small but important repairs.

Dishwater

Slap of the screen door, flat knock
of my grandmother's boxy black shoes
on the wooden stoop, the hush and sweep
of her knob-kneed, cotton-aproned stride
out to the edge and then, toed in
with a furious twist and heave:
a bridge that leaps from her hot red hands
and hangs there shining for fifty years
over the mystified chickens,
over the swaying nettles, the ragweed,
the clay slope down to the creek,
over the redwing blackbirds in the tops
of the willows, a glorious rainbow
with an empty dishpan swinging at one end.

Applesauce

I liked how the starry blue lid
of that saucepan lifted and puffed,
then settled back on a thin
hotpad of steam, and the way
her kitchen filled with the warm,
wet breath of apples, as if all
the apples were talking at once,
as if they'd come cold and sour
from chores in the orchard,
and were trying to shoulder in
close to the fire. She was too busy
to put in her two cents' worth
talking to apples. Squeezing
her dentures with wrinkly lips,
she had to jingle and stack
the bright brass coins of the lids
and thoughtfully count out
the red rubber rings, then hold
each jar, to see if it was clean,
to a window that looked out
through her back yard into Iowa.
And with every third or fourth jar
she wiped steam from her glasses,
using the hem of her apron,
printed with tiny red sailboats
that dipped along with leaf-green
banners snapping, under puffs
of pale applesauce clouds
scented with cinnamon and cloves,
the only boats under sail
for at least two thousand miles.

Father

May 19, 1999

Today you would be ninety-seven
if you had lived, and we would all be
miserable, you and your children,
driving from clinic to clinic,
an ancient, fearful hypochondriac
and his fretful son and daughter,
asking directions, trying to read
the complicated, fading map of cures.
But with your dignity intact
you have been gone for twenty years,
and I am glad for all of us, although
I miss you every day—the heartbeat
under your necktie, the hand cupped
on the back of my neck, Old Spice
in the air, your voice delighted with stories.
On this day each year you loved to relate
that at the moment of your birth
your mother glanced out the window
and saw lilacs in bloom. Well, today
lilacs are blooming in side yards
all over Iowa, still welcoming you.

Pearl

Elkader, Iowa, a morning in March,
the Turkey River running brown and wrinkly
from a late spring snow in Minnesota,
a white two-story house on Mulberry Street,
windows flashing with sun, and I had come
a hundred miles to tell our cousin, Pearl,
that her childhood playmate, Vera, my mother,
had died. I knocked and knocked at the door
with its lace-covered oval of glass, and at last
she came from the shadows and with one finger
hooked the curtain aside, peered into my face
through her spectacles, and held that pose,
a grainy family photograph that could have been
that of her mother. I called out, "Pearl,
it's Ted. It's Vera's boy," and my voice broke,
for it came to me, nearly sixty, I was still
my mother's boy, that boy for the rest of my life.

Pearl, at ninety, was one year older than Mother
and a widow for twenty years. She wore
a pale blue cardigan buttoned over a housedress,
and she shook my hand in the tentative way
of old women who rarely have hands to shake.
When I told her that Mother was gone, that she'd
died the evening before, she said she was sorry,
that "Vera wrote me a letter a while ago
to say she wasn't good." We went to the kitchen
and I sat at the table while she heated a pan
of water and made us cups of instant coffee.
She told me of a time when the two of them

were girls and crawled out onto the porch roof
to spy on my aunt Mabel and a suitor
who were swinging below. "We got so excited
we had to pee, and we couldn't wait, and peed
right there on the roof and it trickled down
over the edge and dripped in the bushes,
but Mabel and that fellow never heard!"

We took our cups into the living room,
where stripes from the drawn blinds draped over
the World's Fair satin pillows. She took the couch
and I took a chair across from her. "I've had
some trouble with health myself," she said,
taking off her glasses and wiping them,
and I said she looked good, though, and she said,
"I've started seeing people who aren't here.
I know they're not real but I see them the same.
They come in the house and sit around
and never say a word. They keep their heads down
or cover their faces with cloths. I'm not afraid,
but I don't know what they want of me.
You won't be able to see, but one's right there
on the staircase where the light falls through
that window, a man in a light gray outfit."
I turned to look at the landing, where a patch
of light fell over the carpeted steps.
"Sometimes I think that my Max is with them;
one seems to know his way around the house.
What bothers me, Ted, is that they've started
to write out lists of everything I own.
They go from room to room, three or four
at a time, picking up things and putting them back.

I've talked to Wilson, the chiropractor,
and he just says that maybe it's time for me
to go to the nursing home." I asked her
what her regular doctor said and she said
she didn't go there anymore, that "he's
not much good." "But surely there's medicine,"
I said, and she said, "Maybe so." And then
there was a pause that filled the room.

After a while we began to talk again,
of other things, and there were some stories
we laughed a little over, and I wept a little,
and then it was time for me to go, to drive
the long miles back, and she slowly walked me
to the door and took my hand again—
our warm bony hands among the light hands
of the shadows that reached to touch us but
drew back—and I cleared my throat and said
I hoped she'd take care of herself, and think
about seeing a real medical doctor,
and she said she'd give some thought to that,
and I took my hand from hers and waved goodbye
and the door closed, and behind the lace
the others stepped out of the stripes of light
and resumed their inventory, touching
the spoon I used and subtracting it from
the sum of the spoons in the kitchen drawer.

Telescope

This is the pipe that pierces the dam
that holds back the universe,

that takes off some of the pressure,
keeping the weight of the unknown

from breaking through
and washing us all down the valley.

Because of this small tube,
through which a cold light rushes

from the bottom of time,
the depth of the stars stays always constant

and we are able to sleep, at least for now,
beneath the straining wall of darkness.

A Washing of Hands

She turned on the tap and a silver braid
unraveled over her fingers.
She cupped them, weighing that tassel,
first in one hand and then the other,
then pinched through the threads
as if searching for something, perhaps
an entangled cocklebur of water,
or the seed of a lake. A time or two
she took the tassel in both hands,
squeezed it into a knot, wrung out
the cold and the light, and then, at the end,
pulled down hard on it twice,
as if the water were a rope and she was
ringing a bell to call me, two bright rings,
though I was there.

After Years

Today, from a distance, I saw you
walking away, and without a sound
the glittering face of a glacier
slid into the sea. An ancient oak
fell in the Cumberlands, holding only
a handful of leaves, and an old woman
scattering corn to her chickens looked up
for an instant. At the other side
of the galaxy, a star thirty-five times
the size of our own sun exploded
and vanished, leaving a small green spot
on the astronomer's retina
as he stood in the great open dome
of my heart with no one to tell.

from Valentines

2008

A Heart of Gold

It's an old beer bottle
with a heart of gold. There's a lot
of defeat in those shoulders,
sprinkled with dandruff, battered
by years of huddling up
with good buddies, out of the wind.

This is no throwaway bottle.
Full of regret and sad stories,
here it comes, back into your life
again and again, ready to stand
in front of everyone you know
and let you peel its label off.

Now, from the wet formica tabletop,
it lifts its sweet old mouth to yours.

Barn Owl

High in the chaffy taffy-colored haze
of the hayloft, up under the starry
nail-hole twinkle of the old tin roof,
there in a nest of straw and baling twine
I have hidden my valentine for you:
a white heart woven of snowy feathers
in which wide eyes of welcome open
to you as you climb the rickety ladder
into my love. Behind those eyes lies
a boudoir of intimate darkness, darling,
the silks of oblivion. And set like a jewel
dead center in the heart is a golden hook
the size of a finger ring, to hold you
always, plumpest sweetheart mouse of mine.

Song of the Ironing Board

So many hands lay hot on my belly
over the years, and oh, how many ghosts
I held, their bodies damp and slack,
their long arms fallen to either side.
I gave till my legs shook, but then
they were up and away. Thus the lovely
soft nap of my youth was worn down.
But I gave of myself and was proud.

I was there for those Saturday
touch-ups, those solemn Sunday
sacraments of Clorox in the church
of starch, the hangers ringing.
On stiffening legs I suffered
the steam iron's hot incontinence,
the meltdown of the rayon slacks,
my batting going varicose.

And it all came down to this:
a cellar window looking out
on February, where a cold wind
pinches clothespins down an empty line.
I lean against the wall and breathe
the drifting smoke of memory,
a stained chemise pulled over
my scorched yet ever shining heart.

For You, Friend

this Valentine's Day, I intend to stand
for as long as I can on a kitchen stool
and hold back the hands of the clock,
so that wherever you are, you may walk
even more lightly in your loveliness;
so that the weak, mid-February sun
(whose chill I will feel from the face
of the clock) cannot in any way
lessen the lights in your hair, and the wind
(whose subtle insistence I will feel
in the minute hand) cannot tighten
the corners of your smile. People
drearily walking the winter streets
will long remember this day:
how they glanced up to see you
there in a storefront window, glorious,
strolling along on the outside of time.

A Map of the World

One of the ancient maps of the world
is heart-shaped, carefully drawn
and once washed with bright colors,
though the colors have faded
as you might expect feelings to fade
from a fragile old heart, the brown map
of a life. But feeling is indelible,
and longing infinite, a starburst compass
pointing in all the directions
two lovers might go, a fresh breeze
swelling their sails, the future uncharted,
still far from the edge
where the sea pours into the stars.

This Paper Boat

Carefully placed upon the future,
it tips from the breeze and skims away,
frail thing of words, this valentine,
so far to sail. And if you find it
caught in the reeds, its message blurred,
the thought that you are holding it
a moment is enough for me.

from Splitting an Order

2014

Splitting an Order

I like to watch an old man cutting a sandwich in half,
maybe an ordinary cold roast beef on whole wheat bread,
no pickles or onion, keeping his shaky hands steady
by placing his forearms firm on the edge of the table
and using both hands, the left to hold the sandwich in place,
and the right to cut it surely, corner to corner,
observing his progress through glasses that moments before
he wiped with his napkin, and then to see him lift half
onto the extra plate that he asked the server to bring,
and then to wait, offering the plate to his wife
while she slowly unrolls her napkin and places her spoon,
her knife, and her fork in their proper places,
then smooths the starched white napkin over her knees
and meets his eyes and holds out both old hands to him.

Bad News

Because it arrives while you sleep,
it's the one call you never pick up
on the first ring. In that pause between
the fourth and what would be the fifth,
in the flare of a lamp you've snapped on,
there it is, having waited all night
until it was time to awaken you,
shaping its sentence over and over,
simple old words you lean into
as into a breath from a cave.
And once the news is out, thrown over
your shoulders like a threadbare robe,
you move on cold feet room to room,
feeling as weightless as a soul,
turning on every light in the house,
needing the light all around you
because it's a new day now, though still
in darkness, hours before dawn,
a day you'll learn to call *that* day,
the first morning after it happened.

Swinging from Parents

The child walks between her father and mother,
holding their hands. She makes the shape of the *y*
at the end of *infancy,* and lifts her feet
the way the *y* pulls up its feet, and swings
like the *v* in *love,* between an *o* and an *e*
who are strong and steady and as far as she knows
will be there to swing from forever. Sometimes
her father, using his free hand, points to something
and says its name, the way the arm of the *r*
points into the future at the end of *father.*
Or the *r* at the end of *forever.* It's that *forever*
the child puts her trust in, lifting her knees,
swinging her feet out over the world.

At Arby's, at Noon

Some of us were arriving, hungry,
impatient, while others had eaten
and were leaving, bidding goodbye
to our friends, and among us
stood a pretty young woman, blind,
her perfect fingers interwoven
about the top of her cane,
and she was bending forward,
open eyed, to find the knotted lips
of a man whose disfigured face
had been assembled out of scars
and who was leaving, hurrying off,
and though their kiss was brief
and askew and awkwardly pursed,
we all received it with a kind of
wonder, and kept it on our lips
throughout the afternoon.

Changing Drivers

Their nondescript, late-model car
is pulled off on the windy shoulder,
its doors flung wide, and the driver
gets out, gripping the roof with a hand
and lifting himself just as the woman
gets out of her side, each of them stiff,
each kneading the small of the back,
rolling their heads on their necks,
squinting into the midday sun.
Then the driver starts out around
the front bumper, swinging his legs
as if they weren't his, his thin hair lifting,
just as the woman straightens herself
and sets out around the trunk, holding
her permanent's white curls in place
with both hands, both man and woman
calling a few words back and forth
across the axis of the car's hot roof
as they stoop and fit themselves inside
and the car's springs settle a little,
and each of them reaches a long way out
to pull the doors shut, her door first
then his, and they rock and shift,
fastening their belts, then both of them
lean forward, almost simultaneously,
and peer into their side-view mirrors
to see whatever is bearing down
from wherever they've been, and together
they ease out over the crunching gravel
onto the highway and move on.

Two

On a parking lot staircase
I met two fine-looking men
descending, both in slacks
and dress shirts, neckties
much alike, one of the men
in his sixties, the other
a good twenty years older,
unsteady on his polished shoes,
a son and his father, I knew
from their looks, the son with his
right hand on the handrail,
the father, left hand on the left,
and in the middle they were
holding hands, and when I neared,
they opened the simple gate
of their interwoven fingers
to let me pass, then reached out
for each other and continued on.

Opossum

You were not at all startled to see me
when I snapped on a light in the barn
and caught you with your curled tail
clutching a bundle of pin oak leaves
you'd been out collecting for your nest
under the floor. In a brain no bigger
than a pumpkin seed, there's not much room
for fear, and none for self-admiration,
so I have pushed aside some of my own fear
to admire you. You have soft fur
like milkweed down, and bright black eyes
alive with all of the big and little things
you've learned from midnight, using
your soft pink nose and your restless
pink fingers. It is those fingers that might
make a person fear you, for they seem
almost human, greedy and dangerous.
I think you may know this, because you
slowly turned toward me and lifted
one of your hands to show me how it could
grasp and squeeze a tiny piece of the light
that fell between us, and even a piece
of my breath.

A Visitant at Five A.M.

It was there on the arm of my rocker
when I turned on the floor lamp,
a tiny moth clipped from the edge
of the night before, gray upon gray
like a dirty city, wings coated with odors
and noise, the beep of a backing truck,
the smells from a seafood restaurant,
waxy sweetness of lipstick. And as soon
as the light grew strong enough to lift it
it was gone, smoke to the shadows,
taking with it the fur collar that brushed
my cheek, a wisp of hair across my lips,
the request that the band never played,
and it was morning, and the house was cold.

A Jonathan in Spring

For Maxine Kumin

An apple tree may live about as long
as a horse, and our old Jonathan,
now rickety and lame with foot rot,
must surely be close to its end, but today
it leans into yet another March,
wheezing with bees. Each spring we think
we've seen the last of its cedar-spotted,
tart abundance, then September arrives
and there in the dewy, leafy grass
lie those familiar, rusty harness bells,
and as they drop around us we can hear
the youthful sound of galloping.

Sundial

Two friends, dead now for many years,
bought it for us one Christmas,
picked it out of a Crate & Barrel catalogue
and had it shipped with a little card
with love in someone else's hand,
a perfunctory gift, as ours to them
must surely have been, perhaps a local
cheese, a few small jars of jam or jelly,
not gift so much as habit, like a handshake,
touch and go, and for years it has lain
on the earth in our garden, telling time
to no one but the fallen curls of leaves
from the ornamental crab, its gnomon
a cattail standing in a pond of bronze,
swinging its shadow past a little turtle,
also cast in bronze, forever wading
into the next hour, followed by the rest.

Lantern

In the predawn cold and darkness,
it was only a pinch of light,
not more than a cup of warmth,
as a farmer carried it over the snow
to the barn where his dozen cows
stood stomping, heavy with milk
in the milky cloud of their lowing.
But that was many years ago,
and his lantern has rusted,
its last fumes lost on the seasons
like the breath of those cows.
But at the last he thought to leave
a fresh ribbon of wick coiled up
in the chimney in case it was ever
needed again, a dollar's worth
of preparation. And, getting prepared
for a later winter, a pregnant mouse
was able to squeeze through a vent
and unravel that wick and make
a cottony nest with dusty
panoramic windows, and there to raise
her bald and mewling, pissy brood,
and then for them to disappear,
the way we all, one day, move on,
leaving a little sharp whiff
of ourselves in the dirty bedding.

A Mouse in a Trap

A tiny wood raft was afloat
on the cold gray sea
of the cellar floor, and to it
a dead mouse clung,
trailing its legs and tail, the ship
of the rest of its life
swallowed up without leaving
so much as a ripple.
I felt the firm deck of the day
tilt just a little, as if all of us
living, surviving, had rushed
to one side to look down.

Zinc Lid

It's the gray of canning-season rain,
neither cool nor warm, and mottled
with feeble light. There's a moony
milk-glass insert ringed by rubber
and a dent where somebody rapped it
to break the seal. But its cucumber
summers, dill and brine, are over.
No more green mason jars cooling,
no generations of dust beneath
the cellar stairs, the ancient quarts
of tomatoes like balls of wax,
the pickles slowly going gray
as kidneys, pale applesauce settling
out of its syrup. Today, on a bench
in a dark garage it's upside down,
a miniature galvanized tub adrift
on time, and in it two survivors,
a bolt that once held everything
together, season in and season out,
and a wing nut resting its wings.

At a Kitchen Table

Not a flock of stories,
not usually,
but a few that arrive at dusk,
in pairs, quietly
creating themselves
in the feathery light.
And rarely with fancy plumage
of blue or green or red
but plain, as of clay or wood,
with a plain little song.
Theirs are the open wings
we light our table by.

A Morning in Early Spring

First light, and under stars
our elm glides out of darkness
to settle on its nest of shadows,
spreading its feathers to shake out

the night. Above, a satellite—
one shining bead of mercury
bearing thousands of voices—
rolls toward the light in the east.

The Big Dipper, for months left
afloat in a bucket of stars,
has begun to leak. Each morning
it settles a little into the north.

A rabbit bounces over the yard
like a knot at the end of a rope
that the new day reels in, tugging
the night and coiling it away.

A fat robin bobs her head,
hemming a cloth for her table,
pulling the thread of a worm,
then neatly biting it off.

My wife, in an old velour robe,
steps off a fifty-yard length
of the dawn, out to the road
to get the newspaper, each step

with its own singular sound.
Each needle in the windbreak
bends to the breeze, the windmill
turns clockwise then ticks to a stop.

No other day like this one.
A crocus like a wooden match—
Ohio Blue Tip—flares in the shadows
that drip from the downspout.

This is a morning that falls between
weathers, a morning that hangs
dirty gray from the sky,
like a sheet from a bachelor's bed,

hung out to dry but not dry yet,
the air not warm or cool,
and my wife within it, bearing the news
in both hands, like a tray.

Along the road to east and west,
on the dark north side of fence posts,
thin fingers of shadowy snowdrifts
pluck and straighten the fringe

on a carpet of fields. Clouds float in
like ships flying the pennants of geese,
and the trees, like tuning forks,
begin to hum. Now a light rain

fingers the porch roof, trying
the same cold key over and over.

Spatters of raindrops cold as dimes,
and a torn gray curtain of cloud

floats out of a broken window
of sky. Icy patches of shadows
race over the hills. No other day
like this one, not ever again.

Now, for only a moment, sleet
sifts across the shingles, pale beads
threaded on filaments of rain,
and the wind dies. A threadbare

pillowcase of snow is shaken out
then draped across the morning,
too thin to cover anything for long.
None other like this.

All winter, the earth was sealed
by a lid of frost, like the layer
of paraffin over the apple jelly,
or the white disk of chicken fat

on soup left to cool, but now,
in cold tin sheds with dripping roofs,
old tractors warm their engines,
burning the feathery mouse nests

from red exhausts, rattling the jars
of cotter pins, shaking gaskets
on nails and stirring the dirty rags
of cobweb. And young farmers

who have already this morning
put on the faces of ancestors
and have shoved the cold red fists
of grandfathers, fathers, and uncles

deep in their pockets, stand framed
in wreaths of diesel smoke,
looking out over the wet black fields
from doors that open into spring.

In first light I bend to one knee.
I fill the old bowl of my hands
with wet leaves, and lift them,
a rich broth of browns and yellows,

to my face, and breathe the vapor,
spiced with oils and, I suspect,
just a pinch of cumin. This is my life,
none other like this.

Sleep Apnea

Night after night, when I was a child,
I woke to the guttering candle
of my father's breath. It made a sound
like the starlings that sometimes
got caught in our chimney, a chirping
that would gradually, steadily build
to a desperate, flat slapping of wings,
then suddenly drop into silence,
into the thick soot at the bottom
of midnight. No silence was ever
so deep. And then, after maybe
a minute or two, I would hear
a twitter as he came to life again,
and could at last take a breath for myself,
a sip like a toast, lifting a chilled glass
of air, wishing us courage, those of us
lying awake through those hours,
my mother, my sister and I, who each night
listened to death kiss the fluttering lips
of my father, who slept through it all.

Deep Winter

In the cold blue shadow behind a shed,
among young ash and mulberry trees
standing in discarded tires, and next to
a roll of used and reused sheep wire
and a sheaf of rusty posts, I am alone
among the others who have stood here,
as they looked out over the snowy fields,
holding their breath against the stillness,
against our awareness of each other,
whole generations empty between us
like gaps between saplings, all of us
having come tracking through winter
to look for something to use to prop
up something else, or for a part
of a part, and not having found it,
standing both inside and outside of time,
becoming a piece of some great, rusty work
we seem to fit exactly.

New Moon

How much it must bear on its back,
a great ball of blue shadow,
yet somehow it shines, keeps up
an appearance. For hours tonight,
I walked beneath it, learning.
I want to be better at carrying sorrow.
If my face is a mask, formed over
the shadows that fill me,
may I smile on the world like the moon.

Painting the Barn

The ghost of my good dog, Alice,
sits at the foot of my ladder,
looking up, now and then touching
the bottom rung with her paw.
Even a spirit dog can't climb
an extension ladder, and so,
with my scraper, bucket, and brush,
I am up here alone, hanging on
with one hand in the autumn wind,
high over the earth that Alice
knew so well, every last inch,
and there she sits, whimpering
in just the way the chilly wind
whines under the tin of the roof—
sweet Alice, dear Alice, good Alice,
waiting for me to come down.

Awakening

How heavy it is, this bucket
drawn out of the lake of sleep
with a dream spilling over,
so heavy that on some mornings
you can't quite pull it free
so let it slip back under,
back into the darkness where
the water is warm, even warmer,
but the dream, like a minnow,
has swum away and is merely
a flash in the murky distance,
and the weight of waking up
seems even heavier. But somehow
you lift it again, its handle
biting into your fingers,
and haul it out and set it down
still rippling, a weighty thing
like life itself, in which you dip
the leaky cup of your hands
and drink.

from At Home

2017

Road Kill

Interrupted, the vulture lifts its red head
from a handful of fur and watches my pickup
approach up the road, just ahead of the dust
I'm towing behind me, and it reluctantly
opens its heavy plowshare wings, like a man
who opens his old black coat to show the police
he isn't armed, but it's already too late for
surrender, and he turns and runs, his coattails
dragging over the road as with weary effort
he hefts his hunger into the air and flaps away,
and in my rearview mirror, I watch him fly out
over a field and slowly circle back and sweep
back down, his shadow flying just behind him
through the dust, then both of them folding
their wings as they step down out of the air
and look around, and settle in to finish.

Locust Trees in Late May

Two of them, sixty feet high, with trunks as big around
as fifty-gallon barrels, lean at a corner of the house,
sprinkling their tiny green bur-like flowers
over the deck and during windy thundershowers
dropping their sprigs of leaves, delicate as ferns.
Just weeks ago they hummed with thousands of bees,
a sound like a huge refrigerator left in the sun.

When they were young they had fierce black
two-inch thorns, but they have since grown old
along with us and have tired of defending themselves.
Just now a nuthatch flits back and forth to the feeder,
hiding sunflower seeds in the bald, wrinkled bark,
and somehow a clump of grass has taken root
in a sap-damp crotch six feet above the ground.

Autumn is still a whole summer away, but it will come,
and with it great showers of copper locust leaves
like pennies, but oval-shaped, more like those pennies
a man at a carnival many years ago rolled through
a little machine on the tailgate of his truck
that pressed the Lord's Prayer into them. Each of us
got only one, but these trees give us many.

The Sick Bat

It was right-side up, which was wrong
for a bat, and was hiding its face
in its shadow, its back to the sun.
It clung to a fieldstone sill at the base
of our barn's south wall, ten feet below
a house for bats I'd built and nailed up
years before. I suppose it was trying
to pull itself up to the others—the sill
was black with their droppings—
but it didn't move. For four summer days
I watched it, thinking it had to be dead
but not wanting to touch it, and then,
one afternoon, I brushed it with a stalk
of tall grass and it cried out, not turning
to face what had touched it, moving
no more than the tip of one wing.
In that instant I'd entered a world
I knew nothing of—at least nothing yet—
and I drew back at once. From then on
I kept at a distance. Whenever I looked
it was there, both dead and alive,
and I looked there until it was gone.

Croquet Ball

It has rolled to a stop along one wall
of the dim garage, rolled in through the wicket
of the overhead door, the last sharp clack
of a mallet so far behind it now that only
the imagination can hear it, clacking in over
the clipped, imagined grass. Its pale green stripe—
the green of the handles on old kitchen spoons—
is even paler now, under a whisper of dust,
and the wood has cracked along the grain
so that the cracks go round and round it
like rings on a planet. And perhaps it is
a planet, and not even one of the lesser ones
but something worth our full attention,
and I, while passing through this life,
wheeling my lawn mower into the shadows,
have been the first to see it waiting there.

Barred Owl

He takes whichever seat is available
at the back of the dawn and settles in,
pulling his old gray overcoat around him,
and now and then throughout the morning
he hoots, but softly, like a man calling out
from a dream. None of us could find him
if we looked, but if we hoot correctly
sometimes he'll come, soundless, tree to tree
like somebody shuffling along in his slippers,
eyes burning, peevish for being disturbed,
his claws curled back and hidden in his sleeves.

Nine Wild Turkeys

It seems there's been an intermission
back in the roadside brush, and this family,
wearing their iridescent formal clothes,
is the first to step out into the empty lobby
of the gravel road, the stately tom in the lead,
opening each foot as he sets it down
like a man releasing first one silver coin
from his fist and then a second, his wife
a few steps behind, carefully placing her feet
where his have been, fitting them into
his prints in the dust, and the young ones
bunched in the rear, nervously glancing
right and left, uncertain of what they're
supposed to be doing, shoving each other
as they scurry up out of the ditch, none
to be left behind. To see ourselves
in a family of turkeys is to see ourselves
as God must see us, stopping his truck,
the box heaped up with bags of seed
and manure, even shutting the engine off,
his elbow resting on the sill, all patience,
amused to watch us make our way across.

A Walk with My Dog

My good dog, Howard, turned from our path
and led me down into a hospice for trees,
a shadowy place that smelled of mushrooms.

A few trunks had been covered by leaves
but for an elbow or knee, though most were
waiting, haphazardly tossed here and there

or clumsily stacked, each of them naked
or sparsely draped with coverlets of bark
that looked to be laundered again and again.

Among them leaned an old carbuncled mulberry,
brown as a mummy queen, most of her branches
down, though two with their shoulders broken

swung tremulous and useless at her sides.
Among her roots was a hole that looked as if
it had once made quite a welcome, the bark

pulled up and away, and her hollowed body
had fallen flirtatiously into the arms of an elm,
a slightly younger tree that stood behind her,

and that elm, too, was leaning on another.
It was this hole that my dog had discovered,
and he pawed and pawed at its doormat of leaves,

asking and asking for permission to enter.
Though the opening was dark it was faintly lit
from somewhere above, as if there were still

a little intelligence burning at the top of that
moldy despair. It was hard to pull Howard away
from that grove where all those trees had gone

to languish, to coax him back from the ancient
mulberry queen who would soon lie lifeless, naked
and bald with the others. So difficult for him,

softhearted dog that he is, to be drawn back
out onto the sunny, grassy path we were to follow
home, and at times he glanced back to that

sorrowful, shadowy place, then up at me as if
to say he was planning to go there again, and soon,
but would undertake that visit on his own.

Meteor Shower

Just before sunrise
I counted nine meteors
scratching the heavens,
just little scratches,
the kind a cat might make
while playing with a ball,
a great black cat
and an enormous ball
that glittered, everything
and all of us inside.

New Poems

I

Sewing Machine

My grandmother's Singer had a black treadle
like the grate on a drain that someone had pried up
from the back, and propped it partly open, and left it
like that, so that something could find its way out
and slink away along the wall during the night
while I was asleep. At a cousin's house I'd seen
the twin foot pedals on a wheezy parlor organ, too,
like the lids of boxes, pried opened that same way,
up from the back, at a tilt, and partly full of dusty
music. And I'd studied my grandfather's shoes
with their laces wrapped on interesting hooks,
working the pedals of his four-door Dodge sedan
as he drove into town with me sitting beside him,
on the way to Kuempel's hardware store for nails
to fasten something down. And as I slowly awoke
to a hazy summer morning in that saggy bed
next to the sewing machine, I pushed one foot out
from under the comforter, which smelled faintly
of clay and old chickens and the nearby river,
and looked at that foot, and turned it in the light
and thought about all of the places I might find
to set it down while I'd be living in the world.

Putz

My mother's nickname, given to her as a child,
meant she was always busy, *putzing* with this
or with that. No photos of her as a little girl,
but the past's what we ask of it, and I can see her
in that house that burned down in the '30s,
crawling over a braided rug in the parlor,
hard on the knees, on her way to take a look at
something just out of the frame, her parents
delighted, together on their horsehair settee.

The other day, in a box of memorabilia,
I found a color slide that I must have taken
when she was in her early eighties. She's feeling
her way down over the rocky bank of a stream,
in a blouse and a skirt I remember her sewing,
wearing soft slippers, toes curling over the stones.
She's holding her hands out wide, as if she were
taking the hands of the air for support, as if
she were just then learning to walk, on her way
to the edge, to get a close look at the water.

Memorial Day

We could hear the parade three blocks before
it arrived at our corner, a Sousa march
that sounded like *distance, distance, distance,*
with an occasional boom wadded up in a ball
of steel wool, and then we'd see two soldiers
coming, marching in step, holding high a white,
gold-bordered banner, like the inside
of a lid to a box of cigars, with something
scrolly printed on it. Behind them came
the trombones and tubas, bobbing in waves
like light on choppy water, then more parade,
some of it stomping on naked legs in boots
with flippy tassels. But, for me, it is always
the vets of the Spanish American War
whom I remember best, the last three or four
still alive, in waxed convertibles, phlegmy
old men in ancient uniforms borne forward
into the light of the future, spectacles glinting,
on their way to the Grave of the Unknown
Soldier, where they would each year hear
or partly hear through ears grown big
and soft as wallets, a struggling "Taps"
soon followed by the pops of five old rifles
with the sixth pop always an instant late,
the punctuation at the end of what we'd all,
all spring, been sometimes looking forward to.

A Bottle Collection

Grandmother Kooser had a collection
of tiny glass bottles, the kind for perfume,
arranged in the sun on the sill of a window
partway up the stairs. She'd pass them
twice every day, first stepping painfully
down from her room in the morning, one hand
on the banister, one on her cane, its tip
counting the steps, and then, in the evening,
heavily climbing back to her bed.
She rented that shadowy house, so little
light or color in it anywhere, the furnishings
all grays and browns, with somber rugs
and the black horsehair settee upon which
my grandfather had lain down to rest
and then died. But those bottles brightened
that place on the staircase, with pale pinks
and blues, gay yellows and greens, their
crystal stoppers sparkling, and though much
had been taken from her she had this,
a moment at that window twice each day,
in which she'd pause, and catch her breath,
and sometimes lift a bottle to the light.

The Clipper Ship

There was a cheaply framed clipper flying in full sail
over the sofa, and it leaned just a little into the glass
as if to look down on me lying there bored, and it carried
more sail than anything in Iowa. It looked as if some boy
had broken a lot of white cups and saucers and stacked up
the pieces, just so, so they wouldn't fall off the sill
of that window that opened onto a faraway sea, a sea
that the ship had only recently ripped open, revealing
the world's white cotton lining. That overstuffed sofa
was heavy and brown like a barge, and it smelled like
the one suit in my grandfather's closet, an angry blue
like the sea in the picture, and as I lay there, climbing
the main mast's springy rigging onto a lofty spar
where I could look down on myself, I could see the sofa
slowly sinking, the carpet all patterned with flotsam
slapping against it, and I wondered, as one might wonder,
would the ship arrive in time to save me,
or would I, hanging high in the rigging, wave it on.

Blackout

I was six when the Japanese surrendered
and the nighttime blackouts ended. At last
we could open the curtains and shades, letting
the stale light pour over the sills. Mr. Posey,
our neighborhood air-raid warden, no longer
walked the streets in his white pith helmet
looking for leaks, then stopping them up
with a tap of his stick on the windows.
In those years, the yellow paper shades
had pulls with flat rings about the size
of silver dollars, and when the shades were up
during the day I shifted my head to sight
through those tantalizing apertures,
peering into whatever I wanted to see.
But after the war the world was different,
and the people who made window shades
had better material to work with, paper
that wouldn't crack and leak light out onto
the tip of Mr. Posey's stick, or stripe his
eager face, and they stopped putting pulls
on the shades, so you had to pinch the hem
to draw them down or let them go, the spring
in the roller flapping them up to the top
where they slapped a few times to a stop,
and everything beyond became one looming
square of outside, not just the little piece
I could see through the pull. We had to look
at everything together, once the war was over
and the light let back into the world.

Goldfish

They were part of the life of an old doctor
who lived there, alone in a cut-limestone house
set back from the road. I was there only once,
as a child, and my father had lifted me up
to the sandy stone lip of a bottomless well
brimming with water ice-cold to my fingers,
and held me to keep me from falling
as I peered down into the goldfish, circling
and circling, halfway up out of the darkness,
all of us circling, though I could not have known
it in those days, the goldfish trailing their silks,
the white-headed old doctor, and me as a child
with my hands on the edge, looking down,
my father behind me, not letting go.

A Color Slide

It's an Ektachrome slide of my grandfather
in his early nineties, hoeing his sweetcorn patch
on a hot summer day, the photograph bleached,
the plants like pale green fountains falling
back, a billed cap cooling the top of his face,
bib overalls and workshirt damp and salty
even at this distance, sixty years from then.
He didn't look up to see me there, taking
his picture. He was looking for weeds, not
immortality, but this stamp-sized piece
of color film and three grown grandchildren,
all in their seventies now, have given him
another fifty years to be remembered,
the blink of an eye. And here he is, bent
in his garden, chopping away at his weeds,
reaching out with his hoe and hooking it
into the earth and pulling himself forward,
like a man standing up in a rowboat, a few feet
from the future, tossing a rope to the shore.

Post Office

The wall of identical boxes into which
our aunt Sticky sorted the daily mail
was at the far end of her dining room,
and from the private side looked like
a fancy wallpaper upon which peonies
pushed through a white wooden trellis,
or sometimes like crates of chickens
stacked all the way to the ceiling.
I'd learned by then—I was a little boy—
that a thing can look like one thing
on one day and another on another,
depending on how you might be feeling.
There were times when we were there,
having our coffee and sweet rolls,
when some woman on the lobby side
would with a click unlock her box
and leaning down, peer inside to see
if she had mail, and see us at the table,
Mother and Father, my sister and I
and our postmistress aunt, and call out,
"Yoo-hoo, Sticky! I see you have company!"
and waggle her fingers hello.

Ames By-Products

That was its business name, but everybody in town
called it the rendering works, and it stood in its stink
on the wooded west bank of the Skunk, its parking lot
half full of run-down trucks nosed into carcasses
piled at the downwind side, brown, rank, and bloating.

Through willows that grew on the riverbank I once saw
one of the workers using the dusty flank of a horse
as a bench to eat his lunch, the sandwich wrapper
a glitter of flies on the hide beside him.

Out of a pipe like a piece of gut, a gray-blue trickle
had eaten its way across a grassy mud bar,
and the Skunk brought bullheads lipping up to it,
the fightingest and fattest up and down the river,
and we had fished it all the way from Soper's Mill
down to the high Chicago and North Western trestle
beneath which our childhood was flowing away.

There was a girl in our sixth-grade class whose father
worked at the rendering works, up to his elbows in blood
gone wormy, blue, and curdling, a poor man growing
poorer by the year, blue cotton shirts worn as thin
as window screens along the clothesline in their yard.

She was taller and older than us from having moved
from school to school, and had big, interesting breasts
before the other girls had any, and it made us mean
as snakes. We pinched our noses behind her back,

as if she stank, though she was always clean and combed,
cycling her few good dresses through the weeks.

She did their laundry, hung out the wash, showing
a good part of her legs as she bent to the basket,
and it seemed it was only the two of them there
as we rode our bikes past, over and over again.

She was cool and aloof in our schoolroom, her eyes
disdaining ours, already a woman, inexplicable,
and then one day she was gone, her father's damp shirts
gone from the sagging rope and the screen door hooked
forever over who she may have been behind it.

Helmet

Just under the sandy surface of the past,
not intentionally buried, but as if, on
a summer afternoon, unbuckled in the heat,
its canvas straps soaked brown with sweat,
it had been set aside, an iron bell that rang
one last flat note, an infantry helmet
from World War I that belonged "in the family"
as we would have said, though whose it had been
had been forgotten. I had played with it
as a boy but not thought about it since,
its having been covered by sand and clay
from other memories washing down out of
the years, until only one dented edge of it
showed, underfoot in a dream, and there it lay
as if reaching up as I woke this morning,
and patiently scraping it out with a spoon
I've dug away most of the hardened clay,
pulled free what was left of the straps,
and brushed its salty hollow nearly clean.
I have grown too old to try it on again.

By Flowing Water

He said that he couldn't tell us why,
exactly, but he wanted to live out
the rest of his life by flowing water,
and he'd found a small rock house
from the 1880s that he could afford,
a short walk from the Mississippi
in a little town in Iowa. Cut limestone,
clustered with ancient fossil shells,
windows in deep cool wells, with sills
where you could set the red begonias
he could remember from childhood.
And along the river was a park
with benches where old men could sit
watching the boats push rusty barges
into the locks, and when there weren't
barges to look at, there would be eddies
out on the surface, catching the light,
circling and circling until they were gone.
You've seen them, he said, like something
you'll never, ever know the reason for,
being swept away. Just once, he said,
he wanted his own bed under a window
with begonias in blossom on the sill,
and before nodding off to take a deep breath
of the river, bait buckets and fish scales
sweeping along through the night,
and to be able to hear the soft ripples
from moonstruck eddies coming to shore
as if looking for someone, lapping the sides
of the beat-up, leaky fishing boats

hauled up on the mud, left forgotten,
part in and part out of the water.

An Antique Teacup

The crumpled old newspapers opened reluctantly:
why go over those troubles again? And the cup
that they'd cradled was cold as a handful of snow
after years in that unheated attic. What seemed
weightless had once held a whole neighborhood,
forgotten one sip at a time, not even leaving the stain
of the gossip. Or perhaps it had grown ever lighter
by the weight of each hand that had set it down
empty, each time more empty than the time before,
marked by the inimitable chime of a fine china cup
placed back in its saucer, the same note as the bell
in an elevator as it slowly ascends floor to floor,
carrying a few fading voices up into an absence.

Parents

My dead parents try to keep out of my way.
When I enter a room they have already left it,
gone off to find something that ought to be done
elsewhere in the house, my dad rolling the Hoover,
my mother with dust rag and Pledge. At times
I've heard their old slippers, pattering away
down the hall, or seen for only an instant
what might be the hem of her skirt as it swept
through a door. I leave all the cleaning supplies
where they're easy to find, and they seem to last
forever. "You don't need to go!" I call out
through the echoing rooms, but they've never
turned back. They leave the floors shining
behind them, and remember to turn off the lights.

Death of a Dog

Howard, 2002–2017

The next morning, I felt that our house
had been lifted away from its foundation
during the night and was now adrift,
though so heavy it drew a foot or more
of whatever was buoying it up, not water
but something cold and thin and clear,
silence riffling its surface as the house
began to turn on a strengthening current,
leaving, taking my wife and me with it,
and though it had never occurred
to me until that moment, for fifteen years
our dog had held down what we had
by pressing his belly to the floors,
his front paws, too, and with him gone
the house had begun to float out onto
emptiness, no solid ground in sight.

A Line in the Rain

I was just at the edge of a storm,
the air heavy, damp, and dark,
driving to Omaha to see my doctor,
when I came upon a paint truck
gray as a cloud, spraying a perfect line
along the edge of the road, so white
that it glowed as if lit from within,
as if the truck had filled its tanks
with light and was slowly releasing it
with a little hiss, or perhaps as if it were
opening a crack in the floor of the day
that I was destined to drop through.
I pulled out and around and sped on,
and ahead the road disappeared
into the darkness, just a part of the rain
then beginning to fall, and even though
I switched on my brights and leaned forward,
I could not see whatever might be there.

2

A February Walk

On one of the earliest days of what may be
an early spring, with fifty degrees in the sun
but not a single trace of green to toe up
under the bleached, snow-flattened grass,
my wife and I walk the thickety edge
of a draw, weaving our way through a tangle
of browns of every key and hue, through knuckled
blood-brown sumac canes and out and around
the rusty cedars, bending in under the elbows
of bur oaks, the two of us taking our turns
in the lead, first Kathleen, pausing to hold back
the whip of a low branch for me, then me
out in front, holding a low branch back for her
in the manner of love, we two among so many
browns around and under and above, like the grain
in a rough oak plank leaned up against the sky
or, better, like slats in a basket, loosely woven,
my wife's red jacket showing through a crack.

In Early April

A white spiral of pelicans slowly drains down
out of a pink late afternoon, settling onto a pond
far in the distance, its surface reflecting the sky
like an opening, a second sky showing through
from beneath, the prairie no more than a film
between the heaven above us and another below,
the pelicans all of one mind, gliding down,
none of them beating one wing in resistance,
before passing through to the bright other side.

Roadside

Someone has picked up after it, but it was there,
a half mile north of the interstate highway
where the paved spur ends and the gravel takes over,
a patch of waist-high weeds where what was once
a trailer park has since gone back to pasture.

It was never much more than a start, and it
never got anywhere close to a finish, just a half dozen
second- and thirdhand cheap aluminum trailers
with windows glaring on their kitchen ends
and doors pulled shut on any hope of welcome.

They sat yards apart, dice rolled out and left
where they'd stopped, and a few ambitious saplings
had pushed up under and worked their way in
and were leafing out over the roofs and the lanes
which once led in and under and were gone.

Three Steps in the Grass

To cut his property taxes, the owner
bulldozed the house he'd been born in,
and the moldy chicken house and the shed
where he and his father and uncles
fixed broken machinery, and took down
the useless horse barn, piled the planks
gray upon gray, slap upon slap in the yard
and on a snowy day the following December,
sloshed it with kerosene from a bucket
weighing almost as much as the past,
threw on a match and burned it away.

What's left is a wire that droops in
from the county road to a power pole,
the meter like a dirty drop of rain,
and three concrete steps that lead up
to the porch that's gone, with an iron rail
like a warm leather strap you can grip
if you've gotten wobbly, and if you climb
those steps and peer through the door
that used to be there you may be able
to hear what sounds like people talking
out of sight in a room at the back,
and see at the other end of the hall
the flare of a lightly curtained window
thrown open to what used to be.

Snapping Turtle

A piece of bark fallen into a pond
will eventually soak and sink, but not
this chunk of darkness, floating inches
beneath the surface, in which a cloud's
reflection is dimpled a little, as if by
the touch of a finger, though no one
dare touch it. And suddenly it isn't
an *it* at all, the mirrored water
altogether empty, just as it was before,
no shadow there, a floating cloud.

A Summer Afternoon with Clouds

Some of the lower clouds, traveling in groups
of four or five, appear to be lost, and pace
this way and that, dragging their carpetbags,
their overcoats tattered, the cheap white lining
spilling. A few have stopped to ask directions
of the wind, who is peevish, with too many to
take care of already. Meanwhile, the tallest
clouds, who can see over the heads of the rest,
have spotted their families waiting for them
where the luggage is piled on the far horizon,
and are drifting away, shoulder to shoulder,
the smaller clouds now sheepishly following.
But still there's the sorely overworked wind
stuck at his station for the rest of the day.
He dreams of having just one afternoon alone
with not one cloud, with a few pleasant hours
to enjoy his collection, his big stamp album
spread open, showing the villages and fields.

Nash

For years, an abandoned Nash from the '50s
sat in a pasture near here, pale green like a pod
dropped out of the sky, brown seats for seeds,
the upholstery split, but not enough rain blown in
through the shot-out glass to encourage
a shoot. It had the smell of a garden, though,
with spilled brake fluid sweet as fresh manure.

With its big, fat whitewalls flat, the whole
turned-over rowboat that it was had settled down
over the axles, and the oarlocks, if it had had them,
were sunk out of sight in the sod. It looked like
a bathtub, too, too heavy to roll back right-side up,
its claw feet missing, its outside painted a green
that matched an upstairs bathroom somewhere.

How had they lugged the tub down the stairs
and onto the grass? One step at a time, with two
big uncles on the down side and a nephew above,
crying a warning as his fingers began to slip.
What else did it look like? The overturned oil pan
from a wreck of a rain cloud, raised on a hoist
and leaking drops of coolant from a mile above.

A Marriage

A pair of cardinals were sampling
the round brown heads of the coneflowers
that lean from our house's long shadow
toward the weakening sun, though
there was nothing the sun could do
for them now, after the first hard frost
of an early November, the pink petals
fallen away, their stalks empty pipes
with a few droopy leaves that offered
little to stand on. The birds kept
slipping, and they'd slowly slide down
out of reach of the seeds, then let
themselves flop backward onto the air
where they'd quickly recover and fly
out of sight for a minute or two, then
come right back. The male was working
one side of the patch and the female
the other, and it seemed they had
nothing to say to each other, nor
did I see either of them glance across
to see how the other was faring.
They just went on with their early
winter work, the male on his rickety
stepladder, changing an overhead bulb,
and his wife on a high, shaky stool
in her kitchen, cleaning the cupboards.

An Appearance

It was October, colorful leaves
falling all through the piedmont,
and I had arrived at a campus
hours early. No one was there,
the auditorium locked, not a car
in the lot. Through the glass
lay the lobby, its floor freshly waxed,
two chairs at a book-signing table
draped to the floor with black cloth,
lines of dust on its folds. Doors
were closed to what I supposed
would be rows of upholstered seats,
the seats all up, facing a stage
with a lectern on hidden casters,
wheeled with a squeal to the edge,
and with a single folding chair
placed next to a long introduction.
From that chair I'd be able to see
a few tatters of masking tape
scattered over the stage, marking
all that had happened forever
before, both the good and the bad,
the hand-clapping dying away.
I was always hours early wherever
I went in those years, anxious to put
the many days away from home
behind me. I got back in my car
and drove to the edge of the campus
where driving in I'd seen a graveyard.
Old headstones leaned into the sun,

and I parked and walked under
the trees, and lay down on my back
between two graves, a man and his wife,
and spread my arms to take their hands,
and closed my eyes, and the leaves
settled quietly over the three of us
while I waited for life to go on.

Walking in Fog beside a Lake

First, the flat thunk of a bucket,
and then a man's voice, only a few
unintelligible syllables flapping in
over the water, not able to reach us until
the last moment, then veering away.

Though we were talking a moment ago,
my wife and I fall silent, nor does the man
in the boat say anything more to whoever
is with him. For a time we are held there
together, listening into the fog,

and then a wave, unable to hold its breath
any longer, rolls out of the silence
and splashes its voice on the rocks
at our feet, and the morning starts up
like an outboard and slowly moves on.

The Constellation

I was on my way home from a party,
ten thirty, a dark winter night, no stars,
a few snowflakes drifting down over
the arms of my headlights, which were
searching the back of the darkness,
pulling things out, a mailbox, another,
a cat carrying sparklers. At the edge
of a town, I passed four stars, placed
on the untracked snow in a cold old
churchyard. They were, of course, those
solar-powered lights for marking paths,
though no one walked among them
at that hour. They made up the only
constellation I could see, and though
the dead lay on their backs, and might
have looked up had they wanted to,
their eyes were closed, and not a soul
was finding any meaning in it.

Turning Up the Thermostat

First there's a sound like that of an elevator
whirring to life far below, starting to climb a cold shaft,
then a puff as if someone had blown out a match.
The furnace comes on with a rush, like a river
pouring over a dam, and the house ever so slowly lifts
from its moorings, swings its bow into the sunrise,
and tugs at the knot in the sash of my robe.

A Yellow Rope

A rowboat in snow, a half inch of light snow
already fallen, onto the oarlocks, the side rails,
onto the oars lying over the benches, snow
falling onto the slats on the bottom, a dreary
gray river beneath, lifting the boat just a bit
out of the water, holding it up to the snow,
and a magical balancing act, a knife-edge ridge
of white stretched all along a yellow rope
leading taut to a post on the bank, tying
the snow-covered boat to the rest of the snow.

Hoarfrost

Two days of an icy prairie fog
and every blade of grass, and twig,
and branch, and every stretch
of wire, barb, post and staple,
is a knot or a thread in a lace
of the purest white. To walk
is like finding your way
through a wedding dress, the sky
inside it cold and satiny;
no past, no future, just the now
all breathless. Then a red bird,
like a pinprick, changes everything.

Moon Shadows

All night the moon was a lamp held steady
while an oak, alone on the crusted snow,
composed a long letter, thoughtfully forming
each word in the copperplate script
of its shadows. From a window halfway up
the stairs I watched it at work, the pale blue
airmail stationery smoothed and waiting
and the sentiments coming so slowly
that I grew impatient and climbed up to bed.
And I fell asleep wondering to whom
the tree might have been writing, and why,
and when I awoke the sky was gray
and cold, the sun hidden in clouds,
and the tree was just standing there,
reaching up into a few scattered snowflakes
beginning to fall, not trying to catch them,
but letting them slip through its branches,
and the letter, whatever its message, was gone.

December Morning

Outside my window, snagged on an eave
and lifting lightly on a breeze, was a four-foot
length of cotton string, the dime store kind
you'd tie a package with. So, curious,
still in pajamas, I stepped out on the porch
to pull it down, and frail as a breath, it broke
at once, leaving a tiny kiss in my fingers,
for it was only a strand of spiderweb,
coated with crystals of overnight frost.

3

A Man on a Bridge

Either halfway across or halfway back,
he is stalled between one side of the day
and the other, the dark river, clotted
with foam, flowing down under him,
hands clamped to the cold iron rail
as if he were trying to steer the bridge
upstream, the aluminum paint flaking
under his fingers, his body straining,
so much so that he is unable to turn
to watch a man very much like himself
roll over the bridge in a loaded truck,
and then another man, in a little car
that comes from the other direction,
both of them weighing the bridge down,
weighing him down, too, with their
ordinary errands, while at a standstill,
arms outstretched, he shoves at the rail,
the muscles in his shoulders tight
as he pushes on, against the current.

Arabesque

A tiny ballerina of a man, no bigger than a child,
rides on the back of a garbage truck in T-shirt,
jeans, and fluorescent chartreuse vest, hanging on
to the barre, pointing one foot in its dirty sneaker,
stretching the muscles in that thigh and calf,
throwing his long hair back, closing his eyes, holding
his face to the light, waiting to step down into
first position, there to be joined by an older man,
who comes skipping around from the driver's side,
the two of them now in a practiced *pas de deux*
with the orchestra swirling them on: percussion
of galvanized cans, cymbals of lids, and then all
the instruments joined in one thunderous clamor
as the great chord in the back grinds slowly open,
met by the wild applause of a thousand flies.

On a Windy Day

A man walks away from a furniture store,
carrying a large mirror.

He grips it the way he'd hold back a kite,
its frame edging into the wind.

The man's lips move as he talks to the mirror,
and the mirror answers.

In the glass is a face much like his,
but even more unhappy, ready to fly.

He squeezes the mirror's shoulders,
he holds it at arm's length and peers into its face.

How much they look alike, arguing
all the way to the car.

People We Will Never See Again

Today in a doctor's crowded waiting room
sat a sad little man of maybe fifty,
wearing a baggy black suit, a black shirt
buttoned to the neck, and black work shoes,
his thinning silver hair oiled back,
and he began singing, but softly, the words
to a song that played from hidden speakers
somewhere above our heavy silence,
music we hadn't noticed before he began,
in his whispery voice, to sing for us.

Passing Through

I had driven into one side of a city,
and through it, and was on the way out
on a four-lane, caught up in the traffic,
when I happened to glance to my right
where a man stood alone smoking,
fixed in the shade of a windowless
warehouse, leaning back into a wall
with one shoe cocked against it,
the other one flat on the pavement.
He was beside me for only an instant,
wearing a short-sleeve yellow shirt
and gray work pants, as the hand
that held the cigarette swept out
and away, and he turned to watch it
as with the tip of a finger he tapped
once at the ash, which began to drift
into that moment already behind us,
as I, with the others, sped on.

Laundromat

Although it's abandoned at two in the morning,
an empty white carton of buzzing fluorescence,
there's always the feeling that someone was there
until only a moment before you walked in,
someone who reached up and popped a soap bubble
of fragrance, the last shimmer of color afloat
in this otherwise colorless storefront, then strolled past
the choir of top-loaders and opened their lids,
leaving them open, each of them holding its breath
before singing, two dollars in quarters per song.

Landing

The pilot lowers the flaps and the plane slows
as if pausing to take one last deep breath
of the chilled air of the heavens before wading out
into and then bellying onto the stale smell
of the city, and holding that breath for as long
as it can, the mushy gray trees of the suburbs
rising up from the bottom. And then it lets go
of that breath with a rush, spreads out its wings,
and lets itself slide, with all the passengers
holding on to its shoulders, down the slick slope
into the depths of whatever is waiting.

Piano

It's an upright, a Ludwig, a hundred years old,
and its patience weighs more every season,
maybe six hundred pounds now, up on its casters,
those squealing sopranos, though one of them,
feeling neglected, refuses to sing. Nobody
has played it for ages, and the silence inside
its grand case, carved with brooches of flowers,
has settled like dust to the bottom, though a trickle
sifts out where the pedals' cold ankles protrude.
Under the fallboard the keys lie in half-light
like a long row of coffins, a different note dead,
sharp or flat, in each one. Or perhaps they are
under a spell and awaiting the touch of a prince
or a princess, though no one alive can remember
when the last person rode in on the bench.

Smoke Rings

Those silent exclamations, those soft O's
that puffed out one after another
and then, like rubber bands peeled from the end
of the morning paper, gave up their shape
and floated, slack and twisted, into the future,
those were the next-to-the-last grand gestures
of the pleasures of smoking, before
each cigarette became such serious business,
such a bitter pill. And the grand finale?
That one big ring puffed out and, quickly,
a smaller ring blown rolling through it,
and then through that one, all those years.

Two by the Road

Yesterday evening, driving home on the highway
in traffic, I passed them, on the edge of the city
where a housing development sits back of a berm
with only its roofs showing over the top. A woman
and a small child were sitting in wind on the slope,
looking down at the traffic, the child folded into
the arms of the woman, both wearing thin jackets.
The grass where they sat had been flattened
by snow that had only recently melted. I passed
in an instant, the two growing small in my mirror.
I imagined they'd climbed, mitten in mitten, up
and over the berm from one of the houses behind,
to sit watching the traffic stream out of the city,
the child warm in the arms of the woman,
and the woman warmed by the child. Miles after
seeing them falling behind me, swept away by
the dusk, I kept catching myself glancing up
into the mirror, as if I might find them again.

Richard

The name on the back of the snapshot,
written in longhand, has pressed through
to the front and appears in reverse
as if written in smoke, above a young man
in a jacket, pinching the brim of his hat,
smiling into the lens. He must have been
Richard, the letters more clearly defined
on the right, where the capital *R*
was pressed down more firmly, while the rest
of the letters grow progressively fainter,
swept backward, like a contrail becoming
a feather. Wind lifts a wisp of his hair,
whips his trousers around his thin legs.
Wind's at work in the gray sky above him,
above somebody's *Richard,* from somewhere,
a young man who looked happy that instant,
his name little more than a faint trace
on the sky as he posed for his picture,
but written in ballpoint, to last, on its back.

Brueghel: *Hunters in the Snow*

It's a postcard reproduction, a little too big
for a recipe card, but a recipe anyway, stew
written all over this rustic scene, the snow
white as potatoes and onions brought cold
from a cellar and peeled, the rest all ruddy
brothy browns. It's too late in the season
for carrots, not one dab of that orange,
and tomatoes are still in the New World,
yet to be cooked in Flanders. Whatever's
available here will get dropped in the pot
with a pinch of black pepper, skaters
sprinkled over the pond. Everyone's starved
in this mountainside village, the three bent,
disappointed hunters, drooling dogs
at their heels, the four aproned figures
feeding sticks to a fire in the background,
and the frozen slope now suddenly fragrant
with the dream of rabbit, of chewy legs
bubbling for hours in a kettle. But that rabbit,
so clever, has yet to be snared, and the hunters,
embarrassed, afraid to go home, stomp
downhill dejected, their stupid sharp sticks
on their shoulders. The three motionless birds
perched in the trees are awaiting the scraps,
and the one other bird, a magpie or shrike
just now flying away, will turn slowly around
on the tip of a wing and come gliding back
into the frame, but this when we're no longer

finding so much in the picture and have set it
aside, the bird winging in for the succulent
stew-bones that aren't to be found in the snow.

Firewood

He's one of those people who look as if
they're halfway on the way to somewhere else,
in a hurry when standing still.
Tonight he's not far from his pickup, parked
on the shoulder above him, and he's down
in the ditch with a chainsaw, cutting up
a tree that the county road crew dropped
and left at quitting time. He's come along
just at the right hour, as if crawling up
out of a burrow after sleeping all day
and sniffing the air, all sour with sawdust,
and he's busily gnawing the tree he's found
into lengths that a smallish man can
with some effort stumble up out of a ditch
and tumble into a pickup, making
a satisfying boom as I drive slowly past
and wave although he doesn't see me,
or doesn't want to see me, cap pulled down
as if he's on official business, working late
on overtime, against the fading light
and early chill of early firewood season.

Card Trick

There is nothing so slick as a new deck of cards
tipped out of the box and fanned over a table,
facedown, slippery as panfish, little bluegills,
their backs printed like scales. "Pick a card,
any card," says the magical bachelor uncle
home for two weeks from the merchant marine,
still wearing his watch cap, black as a night
anchored off Reykjavik, a night with a few
stars of dandruff sprinkled over the wool.
Eyes merry and blue, he is eager to show off
his trick. "Take your time, take all the time
you want," he says, his big brown hand at rest
like an island pushed up, the gray thumbnail
big as a radar antenna, but the children know
to take their time, because they already sense
that this is all there ever is, or likely will be
from this uncle, one trick, the only rare treasure
he'll ever bring back from the rest of the world.

Three Shadows

Nancy Willard, 1936–2017

I was reading, holding a book in one hand,
the poems of a woman who had recently died,
and holding a bookmark, a blank index card,

in the other, when I noticed the card cast
three shadows over the page. The light fell
from two bulbs in the track lighting above,

and one shadow, cast by the older bulb,
was weaker than the other. The third
was where the others overlapped, a sum.

Did they represent something, the strong
shadow the young poet, the weaker the old,
and the sum of the two a new darkness

closing over them both? By moving my hand
I could move the three shadows about,
like cards I was dealing, as if I were telling

the book's fortune, a good one, it seemed,
for wherever I placed them, the poems
that lay under the shadows showed through.

A Long Midwinter Walk

Hard walking over frozen fields
like broken bricks and chunks
of asphalt, and my boots make hollow
swallowing sounds as if they are soon
to be sick. Wind burning my face,
fingers bunched in my mittens,
but I can see, a hundred yards ahead,
the tall grass of a fencerow nodding,
with probably what little snow's left
from the last big storm to stand in,
catching my breath. Beyond, there's
another long field and a fencerow
a ghost in the distance, but first
a little rest, with snow to my ankles
and mouse trails braiding in and out
of the grass. Then once again my hand
between barbs on the topmost wire,
pushing it down so as to step over,
and the plucked fence protesting
with its one low note, in that range
of the scale between forward and back.

Waxer

I once watched a man wax a hallway
with an overweight rotary buffer
that he waltzed from one side to the other
by tipping it ever so slightly, letting
the bristles on one side get a grip
on the floor, drawing the big machine
in that direction, then artfully tipping it
into the opposite, letting it lead, letting it
whirl him out over the beautiful shine
that the two of them made as they
swept down the hall, the man always
in charge but cajoling his partner
into believing that she was, stealing
the show while the man merely followed,
the two swirling out over the gloss
from the overhead lighting, gracefully
rounding a corner and gone.

Ted Kooser served two terms as the US Poet Laureate, from 2004 to 2006, and during his second term was awarded the Pulitzer Prize for his collection *Delights & Shadows* from Copper Canyon Press. His most recent collections are *Splitting an Order* (Copper Canyon Press) and *The Wheeling Year* (University of Nebraska Press). Candlewick Press has published his three children's books, the most recent of which is *The Bell in the Bridge*. Two other books are forthcoming from Candlewick, one of which is a collaboration in verse with Connie Wanek, another Copper Canyon Press author. For the past twelve years, Ted Kooser has edited a weekly poetry column called "American Life in Poetry," which has an estimated worldwide readership, both online and in print, of 3,500,000. He lives with his wife, Kathleen Rutledge, in rural Nebraska.

Poetry is vital to language and living. Since 1972, Copper Canyon Press has published extraordinary poetry from around the world to engage the imaginations and intellects of readers, writers, booksellers, librarians, teachers, students, and donors.

WE ARE GRATEFUL FOR THE MAJOR SUPPORT PROVIDED BY:

THE PAUL G. ALLEN
FAMILY FOUNDATION

CULTURE

golden
lasso

Anonymous

Jill Baker and Jeffrey Bishop

Donna and Matt Bellew

John Branch

Diana Broze

Sarah and Tim Cavanaugh

Janet and Les Cox

Mimi Gardner Gates

Linda Gerrard and Walter Parsons

Gull Industries, Inc.
on behalf of Ruth and William True

The Trust of Warren A. Gummow

Steven Myron Holl

Phil Kovacevich and Eric Wechsler

Lakeside Industries, Inc.
on behalf of Jeanne Marie Lee

TO LEARN MORE ABOUT UNDERWRITING
COPPER CANYON PRESS TITLES,
PLEASE CALL 360-385-4925 EXT. 103

WE ARE GRATEFUL FOR THE MAJOR SUPPORT PROVIDED BY:

Maureen Lee and Mark Busto
Rhoady Lee and Alan Gartenhaus
Ellie Mathews and Carl Youngmann as The North Press
Anne O'Donnell and John Phillips
Petunia Charitable Fund and adviser Elizabeth Hebert
Suzie Rapp and Mark Hamilton
Emily and Dan Raymond
Jill and Bill Ruckelshaus
Cynthia Lovelace Sears and Frank Buxton
Kim and Jeff Seely
Dan Waggoner
Barbara and Charles Wright
The dedicated interns and faithful volunteers
of Copper Canyon Press

The Chinese character for poetry is made up of two parts: "word" and "temple." It also serves as pressmark for Copper Canyon Press.

The text is set in Adobe Caslon. Book design and composition by VJB/Scribe.